*How to Talk
with Practically Anybody
About Practically Anything*

How to Talk with Practically Anybody About Practically Anything

Barbara Walters

A DOLPHIN BOOK
DOUBLEDAY & COMPANY, INC.
GARDEN CITY, NEW YORK
1983

Library of Congress Cataloging in Publication Data
Walters, Barbara, 1931-
    How to talk with practically anybody about
    practically anything.
        1. Conversation.   I. Title.
BJ2121.W24 1983   808.56
Library of Congress Catalog Number 82-45618
ISBN 0-385-18334-8 (pbk.)

To my daughter, Jacqueline, who was two years old when this book was written and was very supportive.

Contents

Introduction

When I was a child, I used to love those advertisements in magazines which showed a big, gorgeous man, muscles rippling, chest expanded, who said: "Believe it or not, I used to be a 97-pound weakling—until I subscribed to the Charles Atlas Plan. And look at me now!"

Charles Atlas was a super strong man with even bigger muscles than the fellow in the ad, and evidently a word or two from him did the trick.

Now then, reading this book will not give you a bigger chest or firmer muscles or a smaller waist, but believe it or not, I used to be painfully shy, a 97-pound conversational weakling, uncomfortable in new situations and with new people, and although I yearned to be warm and sociable, I more often came across as cold and introverted.

Then my life changed . . . from being a television behind-the-scenes writer to a television on-camera reporter. As such, I was forced to take those questions in my head that I had written for others and put them in my own mouth. I learned in time . . . sometimes by just expressing my own curiosity, sometimes by trial and error . . . how to talk to practically anybody about practically anything.

Twelve years ago (ye gods, is it that long!) I decided to try to put my professional and personal experience into a form that could help not only those interested in a career in journalism but also aid those millions of us (indeed, I think almost anybody) who ever wanted to have better conversations, to meet new people, to talk to celebrities, and to avoid being bored or boring. The result was this book. My little girl was only two years old then, and I was working very hard on "The Today Show," so I didn't have a lot of time to gallivant around the country plugging the book. But, to my great surprise and pleasure, the book took off anyway. Perhaps, and I hope it's the reason, because the advice works. The book has stayed in print all these years and, indeed, is now a fixture in many high school and college libraries.

Although some of the people I wrote about are no longer quite so famous or, in some cases, are no longer even alive, the techniques and the experiences are still the same. People are people. We are all a bit shy. We all want to reach out and touch somebody and make an impression, hopefully the best one.

So now, thirteen years later, we are re-releasing the book with the basic material unchanged.

As for me, the 97-pound verbal weakling, I've put on some weight. I sleep later in the mornings and work at a different television network, but I still spend most of my time asking questions and, when I'm lucky, getting some answers. My career has taken me all over the world and enabled me, to my astonishment and great joy, to witness some of the most exciting and moving historical experi-

ences. I've argued for five hours straight with Cuba's Fidel
Castro, conducted the first interview ever between an Egyptian President, Anwar el Sadat, and a Jewish Prime Minister, Menachem Begin. I interviewed the late Shah of Iran
when he was arrogant and powerful, and again when he was
confused and frightened. I've been freezing on Ronald
Reagan's ranch in California and sweltering in Yasir
Arafat's hideaway in Lebanon. I conducted the first interview Iraq's strongman President Saddam Hussein ever gave
to U.S. television, and sadly the last interview John Wayne
ever gave. And I write this introduction on a plane on my
way to interview Clint Eastwood.

My Lord, I'm lucky and I know it. But perhaps my
daughter has summed it up best. I happened to walk into
her room early one evening while she was talking to a
friend, and I heard her say: "My Mummy can't drive a car,
you know. My Mummy can't fix a fuse. My Mummy burns
the meat loaf. Come to think of it, my Mummy really can't
do anything but talk!"

B.W.

New York City
September, 1982

*How to Talk
with Practically Anybody
About Practically Anything*

how to talk to...
The Celebrity

Celebrities used to be found in clusters, like oysters—and with much the same defensive mechanisms. They could be located geographically by sightseeing bus (*And over here, on your right, David Niven's home, Cirrhosis-by-the-Sea*), or by paying the staggering price of a meal in one of the currently "in" restaurants. Or you could catch a glimpse of them at movie premieres, blowing kisses all the way from the limousine to the foyer.

But they didn't *mingle*, and no one expected them to. A young actress with a major role in Clark Gable's last film asked him what she should call him. "For the time we'll know one another," he assured her, " 'Mr. Gable' will do fine."

That sort of regality is gone with the wind. These are the days of decentralized movie-making in such unexpected locations as a New England village or a Minnesota airport. Glamorous people now are making lecture tours, sipping tea with the ladies in towns with unpronounceable names. And there are also the writers, actors, and musicians who travel because they are involved in causes: political, charitable, and protest. You'll meet them in campaign committee rooms, or at fund-raising dinners, or when the cornerstone of a new children's hospital is being laid.

When the *Today* program has traveled to different cities or when I have been on a speaking engagement, I have sometimes been so impressed by new acquaintances that, with all sincerity, I ask them to call me if they plan to visit New York. And I think of busy women like Ann Landers, Mrs. Hubert Humphrey, and Mrs. Martin Luther King, Jr., who became my friends after only one day's meeting. We often drop each other notes about our work or families.

You have two choices when your turn has come to meet a celebrity. You can tell yourself you're such a worldly person that you won't bother him, which may mean that you're just plain shy, or else you can approach him gamely and say something. The latter alternative would be your favorite if only you knew of some opening remark so deft and delightful that the celebrity would be captivated by you. That kind of moment is the fabric of many a Walter Mitty dream, but it's not unrealistic at all. Celebrities have to talk to someone while they're waiting for their coffee to cool, and it might as well be you. And you might as well enjoy it.

You can safely begin a conversation with any famous person—or with anyone at all, for that matter—by indulging your natural impulse to express admiration. People tend to say flattering things to celebrities they don't even like, just to get a good look at them, and celebrities are well aware of this, but you're going to be different. Don't gush, don't take so long to say it that the smile begins to hurt his face, and try to avoid empty superlatives, such as *just loved, marvelous, fabulous, fantastic,* and *divine.*

If you're sincere, and absolutely certain of your ground, refer to the celebrity's achievement that most impressed you; he'll be charmed and grateful. But if there hasn't been an opportunity beforehand to confirm it and your recollection of the exact event is the least bit hazy, stick to generalities. Many a celebrity has been maimed by a well-intentioned fan who wanted only to be kind.

The most common mistake is the worst one: the fan has the wrong celebrity in mind. Composers get congratulated for scores they didn't write, authors for a best-seller by someone else, actors are told that their performance in a movie they never made was unforgettable. It's a deflating experience for the celebrity and one that casts a pall over the rest of the exchange, which will be brief.

There's rarely any physical resemblance involved in the mixup. It comes rather from an inclination to file famous faces away under blurred headings, according to nationality or occupation. People will tell almost any English actor that he was splendid in *Lawrence of Arabia,* or any male singer with the exception of Andy Williams that *Moon River* is a beautiful theme, or they'll see Kitty Carlisle shopping in a department store and rush over to tell her how much they miss seeing her on *What's My Line?*

When in doubt, take the safe route of ambiguity and then gently change the subject—as in, "I've always appreciated your work so much. What are you doing in our town?"

Above all, don't ask him for clarification if you can't recall perfectly. It's essence of nightmare when a fan, beam-

3

ing with bonhomie and quite impervious to the misery he is inflicting, insists on groping through his memory fragments for the name of that Broadway show he saw a few years back, the one with the terrific sets, or maybe it was just one set that turned, anyway the whole family saw it and you were just great, one of the *great* performances, if I could just remember the name . . . The hapless actor is obliged to catalogue his entire New York career but he knows in his heart that it will turn out to be a play that starred Christopher Plummer instead.

Richard Rodgers told me of a ghastly dinner he and his late partner Oscar Hammerstein attended in Paris soon after they had written the now classic *South Pacific*. A portly lady on Mr. Hammerstein's right said, "Oh, yes, you're the writer of that new Broadway show. There's one song in it I just love. Let's see, what is it called?"

As she wracked her brain for the answer, Hammerstein tried to help. "Some Enchanted Evening?" he offered. "No," said the dowager emphatically, "I hated that." "Happy Talk?" Hammerstein suggested. "No, I hated that," said the lady. "I'm Gonna Wash That Man Right Out of My Hair?" "Hated that!"

Finally, after three more "No, I hated that's," the lady came up with her title. "I know," she said, "This Never Was Mine." The correct title is "This Nearly Was Mine" and there is a world of poet's subtlety between "nearly" and "never."

Richard Rodgers' advice to his partner: "Next time, tell her you're Irving Berlin."

There's something even more depressing than this sort of thing, when the fan's only grasp on reality is the celebrity's name, and that's when the fan doesn't have a name

4

at all, not even a wrong one. He is not deterred by this a whit. He knows that the face is familiar, but he can't figure out why, and he reasons that he deserves an explanation.

What he usually says is, "Are you somebody?" Now that's a challenging question to answer; philosophers could maybe handle it, or theologians ready to develop the concept that we are all children of God. The abashed performer may try a modest, "No, not really," but the fan will persist. "I've seen you somewhere before, on television maybe? You *are* somebody."

Character actors, with two hundred solid but inconspicuous performances behind them, tell me that it happens to them all the time. It is particularly unnerving for them because when they do reveal their names, the fan often remains as baffled as before. It's a dreary encounter, as I can certify. I'm on the full NBC network five mornings a week, which is a lot of exposure, but I'm by no means an easily recognized person. I'm frequently stopped by strangers who demand, "Do I know you? Are you anybody important?"

NBC News correspondent Aline Saarinen told me of her all-time "Are you somebody?" experience. She was in Los Angeles reporting on the opening of a new art museum. With her was another NBC correspondent, Jack Paxton. As they were standing outside of the museum, a woman approached with joy of recognition written all over her face. "I just love your reports on the *Today* show," she told a complimented Mrs. Saarinen. "Your movie reviews are the best ever."

"Thank you," Aline responded graciously, "but I think you have me confused with Judith Crist."

"Oh, yes," said the lady, and she turned her attention

5

immediately to Jack Paxton, "*But* I'd know you anywhere. You're John Chancellor!"

Almost no person in the limelight is immune to this. Virginia Graham accepted the situation with humor when she titled her autobiography, *There Goes What's Her Name*. And I remember just recently while giving a talk in Springfield, Illinois, receiving a telephone call in my hotel room from a woman downstairs. She wanted the great honor, as she put it, of being in a photograph with me. If she waited in the lobby, would I be so kind as to come down and pose beside her? I said I would, and then she asked pleasantly, "And how will I know you?" I was crushed. It wasn't a very big lobby, she could have bluffed.

There's one other minor disaster area when approaching a celebrity who makes his or her living in front of a camera. *Never* indicate that he looks different than you expected. It's astonishing how many otherwise sensitive people believe they are delivering a great compliment when they say, "The camera doesn't do you justice. You're so much better looking in real life," or that the celebrity looks younger in the flesh, or thinner. The inference is that the performer is deluded in his hope that he looks good on camera—and that's a blow at his professional survival. He must grit his teeth and say thank you, but some of his confidence leaks out. What is even worse is to tell him that he looks better on television than he does in person. Either way, you can't win. Nor can he.

Don't assume from this that it would be a lot easier on all concerned to leave the celebrity strictly alone, thus avoiding all known boobytraps. People with famous faces expect to be noticed and have a stock of gracious responses to help you with the awkwardness you might feel. Most of

6

them would be very disappointed if some sort of flurry of attention didn't accompany their travels.

There's a show business expression which goes, "There's only one thing worse than too many autograph seekers and that's no autograph seekers."

Hugh Downs, who is as honest off the air as he is on, told me of making a personal appearance in a Midwestern city. He had to make a plane and suggested to his host that they leave by the stage door. "There won't be as many autograph hunters there," he said. "Not only weren't there too many," Hugh told me, laughing at himself. "There wasn't one! I've never been so embarrassed in my life."

Sometimes the problem is that we the public think the celebrity will be irritated by too much attention. I used to feel this way and the loss was mine. I remember attending a buffet dinner where Harry Belafonte was also a guest. The other women at the party swarmed around him so aggressively that I decided to reduce his burden by at least one female, and do him the kindness of remaining aloof. Besides, I thought I'd stand out that way and attract Mr. Belafonte by my cool indifference. I could have kicked myself afterward because I missed my chance to talk with one of the most interesting and intelligent performers of our time.

So by all means, take every opportunity that comes your way to exchange even a few sentences with a celebrity. But try to apply old-fashioned good manners in judging what are the proper limits.

As an example of what I mean, my husband and I had dinner one night in a Baltimore restaurant with Johnny Carson and his teenage son, and discovered firsthand why superstars are forced to become hermits. Other diners in

7

the restaurant came over and interrupted our meal more than a dozen times to speak to Carson. Quite a number decided to stand a few feet away and just stare at him as he ate, and one boldly pulled up a chair and joined us. Johnny has told me that this is his idea of all time rudeness.

My husband and I also remember an evening of such inconsideration that we talked about it for days. Shortly after our first astronauts landed on the moon, New York's Governor Nelson Rockefeller gave them a gala dinner in the grand ballroom of the Waldorf Astoria. Invitations were at a premium and the room was studded with the famous from every walk of life, not to mention the astronauts themselves. But Lee and I watched at first in fascination and then in disgust as person after person in this seemingly sophisticated group approached the table at which Frank Sinatra was sitting. When Sinatra wasn't being asked for autographs, he was being besieged by photographers and television cameramen. With bright lights continually flashing in his face, and strangers leaning over with their arms on him, he tried gamely to eat his dinner. He never lost his patience and I never felt more sympathetic or understanding of his plight. Sinatra's only choice would have been to have left the dinner completely, but then he would have missed the evening's remarks by the astronauts and that obviously was more important to him than his own comfort.

What have I learned from all this? I'd make it a rule not to approach any celebrity while he is eating or relaxing at a private dinner. If you want to say something kind, or ask for an autograph, write a message and have the headwaiter deliver it.

(It's a minor point, but it makes a difference: before

asking a celebrity for an autograph, please obtain a pen and a piece of paper. It's a nuisance for him to be asked to supply either.)

There's another kind of public encounter with a celebrity which also should be subject to the ordinary rules of politeness. It's when traveling by plane—you have fastened your seat belt preparatory for takeoff and looked around at your fellow passengers to discover that the one in the next seat is a celebrity. What to do?

Well, above all, be considerate. The celebrity may be in transit from one ordeal of putting out high voltage charm to another that will be even more of a strain on his resources. Perhaps he has been counting on the peace and privacy of the flight to restore his energy and collect his thoughts. By all means speak to him, say something flattering and friendly—and then pick up a book and leave him alone. He'll be profoundly grateful to you if he's tired, and you've established an opening for a conversation when he feels like it.

One recent example comes to my mind. As I've said, my idea of a man who is the ultimate in graciousness is my co-worker Hugh Downs. But even he has his tolerance level and it reached bottom when he was flying to New York from his home in Arizona. A garrulous lady subjected him to question after question. He finally decided that his only retreat was in sleep, and he begged her pardon as he turned his back to take a nap. He was just nodding off when the woman tapped him on the shoulder. Believe it or not, she said, "Wake up, Sleepy Head. There's something I forgot to ask you."

So much for the bad taste department.

Let us suppose that the celebrity you're with has some

time to spend with you and seems disposed to chat. He's your lecturer of the day perhaps, and you're the official hostess; or you've met him at a party and for the moment you have his undivided attention; or he's waiting for an elevator too, and when it arrives you two are the only occupants. You've progressed safely past the opening courtesy of expressing your esteem and he has replied that he is touched by your compliment. Now it's your turn again.

Try something that demonstrates empathy with the celebrity as a flesh and blood person, subject to fatigue and wounds like any man. Chances are, in fact, that he is a more vulnerable person than you are, and basically shy as well. Don't expect that his real personality is exactly like his professional one; the confident, zany, or sexy image that the performer projects to the public is often a piece of fiction. Comedians in particular put on a glittering show while they're working, but may be withdrawn and despondent otherwise.

Most people who succeed in having really engaging conversations with celebrities stick to the areas that can be described as human interest. These have some promise of developing into a two-handed discussion, rather than those kind of agog questions like "You have such a fascinating life, don't you?" which the celebrity can dispose of with one eye on the clock.

A journalist friend of mine, for instance, had a memorable five-minute chat with Queen Elizabeth at a cocktail party because she asked how the Queen's clothes had weathered the previous day's windy visit to an open-pit iron mine. The Queen bubbled as she described her amazed discovery that she had been dyed henna from head to toe, and went on to tell of attempts to brush her hat clean and her worry that her ensemble could be salvaged—"and it was brand new, you know." By expressing her interest in a simple, practical matter, my friend gained a rare glimpse of the real woman under the crown.

The Queen herself is known to practice the same technique. Millions of television viewers saw her chatting with U. S. Ambassador Walter Annenberg when he appeared at Buckingham Palace to present his credentials. And what did the Queen ask as a conversation starter? She'd heard that the ambassador was redecorating the Embassy and asked how it was coming along.

The saving quality in any question you ask a celebrity is empathy. I'm always won by people who want to know about my schedule—what time I have to get up in the morning (4:30 A.M.), or how I manage to get enough sleep (I don't)—because they show a thoughtfulness about me as a person, a woman who must function out of whack with normal working routine. I also melt at questions about our small daughter Jacqueline, and I think most people love to be asked about their children.

I broke the ice with the usually aloof Barbra Streisand by asking how she chose the right nursery school for her young son Jason. Mrs. Mamie Eisenhower relaxed before our long interview by talking of her favorite grandchild Susie. Former Vice-President and Mrs. Hubert Humphrey enjoy talking of their grandchildren, and I spoke so often to them of my Jacqueline that they sent a candid photograph to my home, autographed with affection, not to me but to Jacqueline. And finally, I know that actress Barbara Bel Geddes and I are soul mates although we have never met, because she recently sent me a beautifully illustrated children's book she had written some years earlier, with the inscription *To Barbara Walters, because she loves children as much as I do.*

I would make an exception in cases where the children are older and are conspicuously drug or divorce prone. In such cases, the subject of children is taboo. No matter how much publicity the unhappy facts of a celebrity's private life have received, no one has the right to poke into them, unless the celebrity brings it up. And sometimes, you will find, the celebrity wants to bring it up.

Senator Edward Kennedy touched me deeply when we met, with his concern for his nine-year-old son, Teddy. The senator told me that whenever he had to leave Washington, he made it a point to try to let Teddy know where he was going and for how long. Since the death of his two uncles, the boy worried terribly about his father.

In most cases, though, children are a safe subject. You can ask how many a celebrity has, how old they are, where are they, is he satisfied with their schools. If you're a parent too, you have common ground under your feet and room to be expansive. You can tell him that your child is older, or about the same age, or whatever, and that you have mixed feelings about the length of his hair, or that she collects lame animals of assorted and smelly varieties.

Keep it light; don't open the closet. This is no place to tell about the time your daughter ran away and was brought back by the police, or what the psychiatrist said last week, or the night your son cracked up a car. It's too heavy, too sad, too personal; resist the temptation to keep the celebrity's attention by playing Peyton Place.

Some people seem to feel a compulsion to tell strangers the most intimate details of their lives, their sexual or drinking or emotional problems. Perhaps these are the areas they keep hidden from people they see every day, so they welcome a chance to dump it all on a transient who won't gossip afterward. Maybe too they have a picture of celebrities living such a wild existence that they are beyond shock. Whatever the reason, it's offensive, unfair, and—frankly—boring.

Besides, there are so many more stimulating subjects to explore. Many celebrities today have deep commitments or unusual hobbies outside of their professional lives. Comedian Orson Bean has established an experimental school and has some thoughtful ideas about education reform; Dean Rusk is an authority on Thomas Jefferson; Candy Bergen is an expert photographer; Steve McQueen has a reverence for the art of driving racing cars.

When you've had some advance warning that you'll be meeting a celebrity, you can find this sort of background information from library reference books and biographies, or from newspaper files, or—if he is coming to give a lecture or promote a film—from the tour director or publicity man.

I have a fabulous friend named Lola, and when I talk of her, I always think of the song, "Whatever Lola Wants, Lola Gets." Lola is by occupation a housewife. She has a tall and very handsome husband, four children, but no actual claim to fame except for her interest in people and the time she takes to nourish her friendships. As a result, she numbers among her very close friends such varied celebrities as Alan King, Sheila MacRae, Jack Valenti, and John Huston. Lola and I were recently at a party that Alan King and his wife Jeanette gave in their beautiful Long Island home to honor Ethel Kennedy on her birthday. I was seated at dinner next to Indiana's attractive Senator

Birch Bayh. The senator is being mentioned as a possible Democratic candidate for President and we talked about both his and my views of that possibility. But Lola stole the show and the senator when she was introduced over dessert. "Tell me, Senator Bayh," she began, starting slowly, "how are the tomatoes coming along?" The senator laughed out loud and asked how on earth she knew that he used to grow tomatoes and still loved to. Lola, who now had his complete attention, explained that she knew that he was going to be at the party and that she'd looked him up in a reference guide she had at her house, much as she would study a libretto of an unfamiliar opera before going to see it. She also knew a good deal more about the senator and was so refreshing and complimentary because she had taken the time to do this homework that I lost the senator for the rest of the dinner. But it was worth it for the experience.

Now then, all celebrities don't grow tomatoes and besides, you might be much more familiar with his work than his hobbies. A few cautions. One is to avoid pretending to be an authority when you're not. If you fake a knowledge of painting, he's likely to leave you stranded at once with talk of acrylics and collages and the New York influence, and he's certain to discover that you're a fraud.

Another hazard of conversation about careers is that many people mention only the obvious. They stress the best-known contribution of the celebrity's lifetime, which may not be at all his best work or his favorite one. I'll bet that Somerset Maugham was pretty depressed by people who remembered only his very early triumph *Of Human Bondage*. And there's a story that Norman Mailer, discouraged that people spoke only of his first novel *The*

Naked and the Dead, was ecstatic when John F. Kennedy was introduced to him and said he had liked *Deer Park.* Rachmaninoff, they say, hated his two most celebrated preludes and called them "very bad music."

A humanized and deliberately provocative question has fewer snares. Ask a painter what is the most beautiful thing he has ever seen. Ask a writer how he first broke into print. (And *never* ask how he gets his ideas; that's trite.) Or ask the celebrity where he lives and if he likes it, or where he'd live if he could live anywhere. Ask a musician if it is a waste of time to go to the symphony if the music seems meaningless. Ask him how to inspire children to appreciate music. Ask him if music is an acquired taste.

First thing you know, the celebrity will be talking to this person—you. And you won't just be listening, you'll be talking, too, and, most important, you'll be having a good time.

SPECIAL CIRCUMSTANCES

Two Celebrities at Once: When two celebrities are standing together, as may happen at a cocktail party or dinner, don't fall upon the one who is your favorite and ignore the other; it will make both of them uncomfortable. Say, "I'm so pleased to meet you both," and if you're going to linger, make sure you have a three-handed conversation. If the person with the celebrity doesn't look familiar, and even when you're introduced there are no bells of recognition sounding, make the assumption that the unknown person matters. Put out the same warmth and friendliness toward him as you aim at the famous person.

15

Remember, too, when meeting one celebrity, not to put him down by asking about another more famous person he may have worked with. For example, when Mike Nichols was directing his first motion picture, *Who's Afraid of Virginia Woolf?* the poor man was up to here from answering questions about his two illustrious stars Elizabeth Taylor and Richard Burton. But he gave me one of my best interviews, I think, because I began by saying, "Mr. Nichols, I'm not interested in hearing about Elizabeth Taylor or Richard Burton. I want to know about you." And you know what else? Eventually, of his own free will, he got around to talking about the Burtons.

The Author Whose Book You Haven't Read: Don't bluff that you have read it, and don't apologize for "not having time"—that's weak—and don't tell him you're on the waiting list to get it from the library (his royalties come from sales, not rentals). If there is time beforehand and the book is non-fiction, do what I often do when I must talk with five authors a week. If the book is non-fiction, I read the first chapter and the last, and a few in between. If there isn't time, or I can't get a copy in a hurry, I try to find a review of the book. It is no substitute for having digested the entire book, but it's better than no preparation at all. Sometimes the subject matter can be a springboard for a discussion. If you know the author has written about urban decay, for instance, ask his opinion of what is happening in your city.

Celebrities Who Don't Like to Talk: This includes, surprisingly, those outgoing, funny comedians who seem so approachable that strangers hail them by their first names.

Buddy Hackett and Red Skelton are perfect examples of this. They give the impression that they are gregarious to a fault, but away from the stage, neither is very communicative except with close friends. Alan King is the rare exception to this generalization. He has a wide range of interests from politics to religion and loves nothing better than a stimulating discussion. But very often, highly creative people who work alone—painters, poets, fiction writers, and musicians—are almost unable to relax in a social gathering. Don't be offended and don't be hearty; be gentle and calm and considerate, as you would be with anyone acutely nervous.

The Celebrity Is Black: Many people have a tendency to assure a Black celebrity at once that they are glorious examples of liberal thinking. They tell anecdotes whose main point is that they have Black friends, or that their children bring Black friends home to play, or that they have supported Black causes since the Montgomery bus strike of 1955. Or they ask him his opinion of the Black Panthers, or tell him how shocked they were by the killing of Martin Luther King, or they congratulate him for being a credit to his race. It's all a dead giveaway as far as the celebrity is concerned. As he sees the situation—accurately, I think—he isn't being treated as a flesh and blood man at all but as a representative Black confronting a white conscience. That's prejudice; it's sneaky, but that's what it is. And don't presume because you have a tender heart and have read *Malcolm X* that you appreciate the difficulties of being Black. Unless you are Black yourself, you can't possibly imagine what his life is like. I think that one of the main reasons for Bill Cosby's success was that his humor was the kind any of us had experienced as children. He never stressed the Black. He was a comedian on stage first and a Black comedian only incidentally.

I remember, however, at the other end of the line, an interview I filmed with the brilliant and strikingly beautiful wife of Black Panther Leader Eldridge Cleaver. I approached Kathleen Cleaver with great warmth and empathy as if to convey to her that I was completely open-minded about her cause. I thought that this would lead to a more relaxed and ultimately more probing interview. But Mrs. Cleaver made it clear to me that she was having none of me. Her attitude said "Just ask your questions and I'll answer them, but don't try to pretend that you have any knowledge of what I've actually gone through."

So keep to the same topics that would interest you if he wasn't a Black: ask him if he finds celebrity tours a strain; if he would prefer talking to a male or a female audience; if the celebrity is a woman, ask for tips on packing a suitcase; ask about the children. And don't go overboard with gracious charm. As in "Some of my best friends are Jewish," oversolicitude is patronizing—and bigoted.

The Celebrity Is an Athlete: Most men have no difficulty in talking to athletes and many, in fact, depend on sports for their small talk. Former President Richard Nixon, for instance, is said to use the subject of sports as his ice breaker. To make strangers feel more comfortable in his presence, he begins by discussing the latest football or baseball game and even if the guest knows little about the game, the President's enthusiasm alone warms the atmosphere. But here you are. You can't tell a goal line from a shoelace but you want to talk to the hulking hero anyway. I've had this problem when the *Today* program for reasons of whimsy or "let's shake them up a bit," sometimes will assign our resident sports expert Joe Garagiola to comment on a fashion show and me to interview a football star. But whether I meet the athlete in front of television cameras or at a dinner party, the technique is the same. I begin by explaining that I know he's world famous at what he does, but I must apologize because I know nothing about his sport. Clearly I can't discuss the technicalities of the game, and I don't try, but I am interested in *him*. I can ask what is the excitement of the game for him, how does his family feel about his playing, does his wife worry about his being hurt, does the traveling across time zones upset him, do his children want to be professional athletes and how does he feel about that. And unless it's really terribly funny or in his field, I don't inflict on him the story about the time I got a stiff neck at the tennis matches, or my hilarious attempts to skate. I know he'll be bored rigid.

Almost Celebrities: The near-great live precariously, never quite achieving the warm safety of real fame and always anxious that what little they have may slip away. Their inner fear may show itself as brashness, or quick fury over imagined discourtesies, or arrogance. However difficult the personality, put yourself out to be kind. Treat him with the deference he desperately requires. The lesser his fame the greater may be his need for affectionate treatment.

The Celebrity Is Fading: I'm usually apprehensive when interviewing a formerly great star who is no longer in the limelight. I know that the viewer is curious to learn how the aging actor or athlete is accepting time's attrition, but no one wants to obtain this information at the cost of the guest's pride. The best method, on television or anywhere else, is to put the crucial questions obliquely in the third person. Don't ask Joe DiMaggio how he felt to be sitting in the stands idly while the crowd roared for a younger slugger. Ask him instead to comment on Mickey Mantle's gloomy observation on retiring, "From now on, it's all downhill." In answering that, he's almost certain to draw in his own experiences as illustration. Or ask a once-successful actress what she thinks of Brigitte Bardot's remark, "The best years of my life were when I was seventeen." The attitude you take is that the star is handling himself or herself magnificently, an example to all of how a gradual withdrawal can be accomplished with dignity and grace. You want him to explain why others accept this inevitability with so much bitterness and desolation; the reply will reflect his own insight and experiences in a natural, relaxed way, since he won't be feeling defensive. In interviewing Ingrid Bergman, for instance, I complimented her sincerely on her frankness in admitting her age and asked if she felt that beautiful women in general had a more difficult time than others accepting age. I remarked truthfully to Rex Harrison, "You seem very happy, very much at peace," and he told me that "getting out of one's cradle is a very nice thing," and that he thinks he gets better parts now that he is middle-aged, and that he enjoys growing older.

Keep it positive, avoiding such negative openers as "What do you do with your time these days," or, "We miss seeing you on television. Where have you been?" or, "It must be hard to be away from the stage for so long."

If you really must explore a sensitive area such as a former drinking problem or an old scandal, again be indirect. For example, I might ask an actor who has had more than his share of ups and downs, "How do you feel about the public, which seems to swing from criticism to adulation and back again so easily?"

When I wanted Judy Garland to talk about her difficult childhood, I asked her how young people in show business today compared to her friends in the days when she was starting in vaudeville. And I got an answer that still makes me feel sad every time I recall the interview. "We all started too young in those days," she said. And then she added with a tiny smile, "You know my mother was the stage mother of all time. She really was a witch. If I had a stomach ache and didn't want to go on, she'd say 'get out on that stage or I'll wrap you around a bedpost.'"

The point is that if you ask a performer not about himself but about others, you will very often find that he will respond by talking most personally about himself.

Another tip on the same subject: don't attempt to probe in sensitive areas right after the introduction. Talk about less personal matters until you've built up some feeling of trust and liking. Until the celebrity, or anyone for that matter, feels comfortable with you, it's not likely that he will feel like disclosing anything more intimate than his hat size.

2

how to talk to...
Tycoons

A tycoon is even more alarming than a celebrity, especially if he happens at the same time to be your boss, or your husband's boss. He presents a problem for conversation first of all because he is often extremely rich. This is awesome enough by itself—the thought of money enough to wade in almost unhinges the mind—but it also means that your styles of living will have so little in common that topics such as vacations and house-hunting cannot be attempted.

The range of discussion material is further reduced by your near-total lack of comprehension of what he *does* to earn all that money; stock mergers and the rising cost of industrial chemicals have never enthralled you. There's no basis for conversation at all, or so you think.

It isn't really impossible; with a little help from your stock of poise and grace, you can slip easily into a beguiling conversation with any millionaire. It might help to control your initial qualms to remember that he's almost certain to be a man with some personal charm—you don't get to be president of the company with the manners of a boor, except perhaps when your father was president before you.

If your introduction was cursory, or took place much earlier in the gathering, help him out by identifying yourself clearly and giving some description, as in, "I'm Betty Wakeford and I'm married to Jim, that handsome dog over there with the beard. He's an architect and I'm back in college trying to understand sociology."

An easy conversation starter in such situations is to compliment the tycoon on how he's dressed. Admire his tie, or his color combination, and ask, "Does your wife help you select your clothes?" It's innocent-sounding but it instantly produces two items of interest: (a) whether or not he is married, and (b) something about the quality of the marriage. A man who snorts, "Good God *no!*" discloses that the honeymoon is over.

Don't make the common mistake of trying to talk business with him. It will be dull for both of you, since the intricacies behind the power decisions he makes are probably well beyond your scope. Anyway, business is not necessarily his favorite topic at a gathering where he had hoped to relax. So you will stay on the firm and more fascinating ground of personal interest questions.

For instance, you might try the approach that worked for me when I talked with Aristotle Onassis: ask the tycoon about his very first job. Many successful men have an ardent relationship with their careers and dote on recollections of their first earnings with the same poignancy and pleasure of other men recalling their first loves.

Let me give you a case history of my own conversation with a tycoon who was a total stranger. I had been invited to the one hundredth anniversary celebration of New

York's Metropolitan Museum of Art and was included as a dinner guest at a party given by Mrs. Charles Payson, best known as the owner of the New York Mets. I didn't know the hostess or very many of the other guests, who included, I noticed with awe, the sculptor Henry Moore and the former U. S. Ambassador to Britain, John Hay Whitney.

My husband was away and couldn't come with me, and I had advised Mrs. Payson of this. I found myself seated next to a man whose place card identified him as Sir George Weidenfeld. Well, there was something to go on *right off*. I asked him first how I should address him and he informed me genially that in England he was known as Sir George but Americans usually called him George.

Then I asked what it was like to be knighted by the Queen, and he told me the expectation was the best part. You line up with a lot of others, kneel and are touched lightly with a sword on either shoulder, and it's all over in five minutes with nothing visible to show for it. I asked why he was knighted and he said he was a book publisher. This led me to the Onassis-type question and I asked if he'd always been in that business.

With that, we were really off. Sir George told me with great relish how he'd become a book publisher by accident. He laughed as he said that his first published book was written by an obscure professor who had been his college tutor and had an intriguing point of view about labor. The obscure professor was Harold Wilson, until the last election, Prime Minister of Britain.

So by all means ask him to reminisce about his early years. Was his job more fun then? How did he get involved with the company he now heads? Did he have an early hero? Did the boss make him nervous? If he's a self-made millionaire, ask him how he made his first million—but be prepared to leap to another topic if this question seems to make him uncomfortable.

I still remember the engrossing answer from a simple question I asked a citrus millionaire who was one of our sponsors on *Today*. I was seated next to him at a company lunch, and I knew that our sales department wanted to keep his affection, his interest, and above all, his account. I had read in some quick research I did beforehand in *Time* magazine that he had earned his first fortune while still at the University of Miami, by noticing the great losses sustained by citrus growers through spoilage. He had devised a scheme to put fresh orange juice in cartons and distribute it quickly, and later extended the idea to include packaged grapefruit juice and fruit salad. So I asked him about this talent for ingenuity. "If you wanted to become a millionaire today, how would you go about it?"

He was quick. "I would try to find something needed on the market, something uncomplicated which people don't have. For instance, one of the messiest things to make is bacon. Everyone loves to have bacon for breakfast but no one likes to clean the pan afterward. Bacon perhaps could be dropped in the toaster with a paper lining underneath to absorb the grease. After it's finished, you throw away the greasy liner."

Don't you prefer that sort of reply to the one which results from tycoon-type questions such as "How does the new political administration affect you?" or, "What is happening to our economy—is it going up or down?" or, "How many black people are you hiring now?" These blockbusters only work when you are informed yourself in the areas you bring up, and have a genuine eagerness to hear his ideas.

Nostalgia offers the best opportunity for good conversation but if he isn't inclined to unpack his reminiscences, ask him if he has a desk (many tycoons nowadays work in offices that resemble living rooms) and what he keeps on his desk. Or ask about his working hours—they'll be brutal, which is why you're not going to ask right off about his children. Or ask him how he handles the strain of his heavy responsibilities, how does he relax?

And if there's a pause along the way, try to resist the temptation to fill it by giving him your helpful hints about his product. Heads of airlines will turn glassy-eyed if you decide to unburden yourself of your ghastly experience in one of their Chicago-bound planes, and restaurant owners can survive without your ideas for improving the service. It is particularly wise to hold back the advice when talking to someone in show business, about which it has been said, "Everybody has two lines of work—his own, and show business."

My husband Lee Guber is a theatrical producer, so I'm aware of how tedious and frequent are the offers of "great ideas" for plots, or casting. Johnny Carson now avoids parties with people he doesn't know well because he is always cornered by someone with a suggestion about a guest he should put on his show right away or criticism of some guest on a previous show. People offer me the same kind of assistance in casting the *Today* show guests, but I'm able to get off the hook by saying, truthfully, that I have nothing to do with the selection of guests—it's in the hands of the producer.

But it may be that you do have a really valid comment to make about the tycoon's business that you're certain will interest him. You've turned it over in your mind a few times, hesitating whether or not to bring it up, but the conversation has proceeded long enough for you to observe that the tycoon is an alert and perceptive man, and he may have formed a similarly favorable impression about you. So you decide to plunge ahead.

Even so, don't hit him on the head with it, as in, "I've been wondering whether I should tell you, but maybe you should know that the packaging on that dishwasher soap of yours is terrible. Brinks couldn't do a better job of protecting it—*no one* can open that box."

If it's that bad, he already knows about it and he's headed a dozen meetings to change the situation and maybe discovered that it isn't feasible to remedy it for a long time. Or maybe this is the first complaint he's ever heard about it, which makes him decide on the spot that you're a crank. In any case, you've put him on the defensive and he can't help but be nettled.

Instead, put it this way: "One of the reasons I'm so pleased to meet you is that you're the one person who can give a knowledgeable answer to a question that's been bothering me for months. I've noticed that some of the companies that make soap for dishwashers package it in heavy wrapping that's really difficult to open, and I've wondered why." You've made the same point, but with a big difference. This way you show you are sympathetic with the problem from his point of view, and you haven't singled out his product. You're asking for information without implying that he isn't competent. He's glad to tell you about it, because you're a listener and not a combatant.

It's the same ballgame, with the same rules, when you're talking to any businessman. The owner of your local shoe store or the bank manager on the corner feel the same pangs over the wellbeing of their establishments as any tycoon does about his empire—or any mother about her babies, for that matter. Don't confuse being stimulating with being blunt: a question about how he keeps his place attractive with so many people coming and going brings out the same answer as the question, "Why is your place always such a mess?"—but you haven't shafted the man in the process.

A conversation isn't a competition. Businessmen spend their working days, and a lot of sleepless nights, comparing their own accomplishments with those of other men. It's the price of survival, and some thrive on it, but it's a blissful change to talk to someone who doesn't seem an adversary. See if you can discover what in his life gives him pride, where he feels accomplished and valuable. He'll bloom before your very eyes, and you'll both have a marvelous time.

And don't be a blob yourself. Tell him about *your* good memories and *your* interests. If you ask him about the first day he arrived at his new service station or supermarket and if he felt exhilarated, tell him about how you felt the first time you had a key to your own home. You're a person too, and also valuable.

The Tycoon Is a Lady: This is not unusual any more, and rapidly becoming commonplace as women today gain recognition for organizational skills. Some have taken over the business on the death of their husbands, and developed into able administrators under that kind of pressure; more frequently, the lady started in a minor job and demonstrated so much sheer skill and judgment that promotion was inevitable.

Either way, the image of the lady tycoon is too often a merciless one. There's a myth that she succeeds by means of jungle tactics, that she's a ruthless, predatory, castrating monster. Women, as often as men, are likely to be prejudiced against her. I think she represents a particular affront to those women who make a full-time occupation out of being ornamental and helpless . . . and to those men who are afraid that their wives may grow restless.

If you are among those who share the kind of bias that gives the women's liberation movement ample fuel for its steam, get a grip on your tone before you open your mouth to talk to a woman tycoon. She's sensitive to antagonism—she's faced it all her working life—and she'll be hurt and dismayed. Besides, she may be indignant enough to retaliate and, sweetly-smiling, cut you off at the knees. There's flint in her, of course; she couldn't be a decision-maker otherwise.

There's a line in George Bernard Shaw's *Pygmalion* that applies here, when Eliza Doolittle explains, "the difference between a lady and a flower girl is not how she behaves, but how she's treated." Treat the lady tycoon like a lady, and you'll find her gracious and pleasing; treat her like a sweaty gladiator and you'll get a sword in your ear.

In fact, most of the time, curiously enough, the lady tycoon is much *more* feminine and fragile seeming than her housewife counterpart. It may be that really threatening women, the kind who match the misconception about lady bosses, are passed over for promotion and leadership. Whatever the reason, I find that the lady tycoon who achieves the most gives the appearance of being absolutely guileless.

Helen Gurley Brown, for instance, the editor of *Cosmopolitan* magazine and author of *Sex and the Single Girl*, talks so softly she makes Jacqueline Kennedy Onassis sound like a stevedore. She bats long eyelashes at you, usually sits quietly with her hands in her lap, and gives the impression that not only is it impossible that she could control an entire editorial staff of both men and women, but that it is only by valiant effort that she's able to speak up at all in this small group. This almost wispy, little-girl quality is also true of such other women tycoons as advertising's crack Mary Wells and the former president of Bonwit Teller, Mildred Custin.

But you do want her to speak up and the relevant personal question is again the best approach. Asking her how she manages her personal life is always a much better gambit than wading into a heavy discussion of her career. Ask the simple questions that you're curious about, but mind your manners—her hide is no thicker than yours. For example, "Is it very difficult adjusting a job like this to your marriage?" or, "Are you a morning person or does your energy peak later in the day?" or, "How do you find time for the grooming chores—having your hair done and your clothes fitted?" or, "Do you have to eat out all the time?" or, "Can you take a vacation whenever you like?" If she has children the very best question you can ask is about them.

The same questions that intrigue male tycoons are likely to work with her as well. Like him, she's reached the stage of romanticizing her early struggles and has a fine time relating them in a haze of pink. Help her to avoid actual dates, however; only one-hundred-year-old men are proud of growing old.

Don't make the error that women's clubs regularly commit when they have a prominent woman for a guest. Invariably the ladies will barrage her with woman-in-a-man's-job questions, which thinly disguise animosity. To my mind, there's a double message coming across in questions like "Do men resent you?" (the suggestion being that they do, and rightly) or, "How do you keep your femininity?" (the inference is that it must be a grim and losing battle) or, "Do you like to have men working for you?" (which implies clearly that of course you do, you tough old bat). Don't play feline games.

The Tycoon's Wife: Many a tycoon's wife has been made aware over the years that she's a social inconvenience. Mr. Big is married so she must be invited too, but no one really is interested in her or knows how to talk to her. She's either ignored as much as decency permits or else is required to respond with fresh delight to one hundred variations of the question, "What's it like to be married to him?" These wives often develop stock phrases,

32

offered with a smile: "Who me? I'm only a woman," they say, or, "Don't ask me, I only came along for the ride." What they mean to convey, somewhat bitterly, is that they're prepared to be overlooked.

You can become the most unforgettable person the tycoon's wife ever met by showing that you want to talk to her about herself, as a separate and exciting person. She must have unique qualities, after all: he's an astute man and he picked her. So try going back to the beginnings. Ask her how she met her husband; ask what she was planning to do with her life before she met him; ask what kind of temperament and adaptations are required of the wife of such a man; ask if she recognized qualities of greatness in him when she first met him.

Or ask how she arranges her personal life with such a dynamo around the house. How does she schedule things so the children have some time with him? Is it difficult for the children, especially sons, when their father is so prominent and important? Does she have a hobby or charity that she pursues on her own? What advice would she give other wives in her position?

When I asked Mrs. John Lindsay that last question, she replied somberly, "She'd better love being married to a politician, or learn to love it, or else she'll have a very hard life."

It was a similar question which led to a revealing conversation with Mrs. Dwight D. Eisenhower one sweltering afternoon in Gettysburg. I had gone there to interview her and the former President on the occasion of their fiftieth wedding anniversary. The other networks had also sent television crews, but I was the only woman present. When I had finished my interview with the couple, Mrs. Eisen-

33

hower thoughtfully invited me inside the farmhouse for some iced tea and woman talk, arranging to send cold Cokes out to the men.

As we were settling into chairs, I asked, "Your husband's life is so busy and complicated—how do you arrange your own life so that you have time for yourself and for him?" And then she went through her day's routine, telling me that she got up early in the morning, had breakfast downstairs and then usually returned to bed to answer her mail and go through menus. She had an inner ear imbalance, so she generally stayed in bed until lunch and then went downstairs just as her husband was returning from his round of golf.

She took pains, she said, to make certain that any unexpected guests he brought with him would feel welcome; she regarded it as important that he was able to bring people home for lunch, even without warning her.

I asked her the secret of a happy marriage. She replied with a mischievous grin, "I can't speak for any other marriage, but the secret of our marriage is that we have absolutely nothing in common."

The rest of the conversation was on this same note of warm intimacy and I remember in particular her delight in the Gettysburg farmhouse, the first real home she had had throughout her marriage. Everywhere else she and the General lived, from Army bases to the White House, the roof was a temporary loan.

I am especially grateful that several years later Mrs. Eisenhower still remembered so well the easy comfortable way we talked that day that she granted me her only television interview after her husband's death.

And it began because I asked about *her*. I would only

add that this same focus is also the most tactful and rewarding when talking to any relative of a famous person. Don't ask, "What's your famous son really like?" Ask, "What qualities did you most want to instill in your children?"

The mother of Martin Luther King, Jr., gave me a memorable answer to that very question. She said, "We lived by the theory of the three S's. If our children had some money, one-third of it was for Spending, one-third was for Saving, and one-third was for Sharing with the church or some other worthy cause." Her son, you recall, gave away his entire Nobel Prize award money to the civil rights movement.

If you are introducing the child of a famous person, skip the references to the relationship. They need all the help they can get to keep their identity separate from overwhelming parents. I almost blundered one time on the *Today* program when I was coyly preparing to introduce Marlo Thomas as "Danny Thomas's little girl." She asked me politely not to—she had been acting for ten years, she pointed out, and while she was proud to be Danny Thomas's daughter she definitely couldn't see herself as his "little girl."

The Tycoon's Husband: The cardinal rule here is to get his name right. The lady tycoon may be using her single name, or the name of a previous husband, because she established her reputation at that period of her life and can't switch it. Never assume that his name is the same as hers; always check. And when he has accompanied her to a party or meeting, use her married name. I much prefer hostesses who say, "I'd like to introduce you to Arlene and Martin Gabel" or "This is Arlene Francis Gabel and Martin Gabel," rather than "This is Arlene Francis and Martin Gabel"; and I find it tactful when my place card at a dinner where my husband is present reads "Mrs. Lee Guber" or "Barbara Walters Guber." (If the married lady tycoon arrives without her different-name husband, ask her how she wants to be introduced; her preference may depend on the type of gathering it is.) Later when talking to the husband of a well-known woman, avoid bombarding him with questions about her. Some men are unruffled by the inference that their wives are better known than they are, but such jewels are rare. My husband is one . . . a blue-white diamond. More commonly, men married to successful wives are pained by being treated with indifference or regarded as dull appendages. So ask questions about *him*, what he does, how he got started, his views on space exploration.

Don't on being introduced hint archly that his marriage must pose unusual difficulties; you're insulting them both at one blow. I remember the first time my husband and I were introduced to David Susskind. Mr. Susskind started with, "Oh, you're that girl on the *Today* show," and followed this up with, "My wife used to do that show—but I don't let her work now. One ego in the family is enough." He had managed to destroy me and castrate my husband in less than thirty seconds, but he had been so blatantly self-involved that it didn't hurt at all. Lee and I looked at one another and, at the same time, broke into laughter.

The Tycoon Is a Doctor, Lawyer, Architect, etc: Word seems to have gotten around, luckily, that it is improper to ask for free professional advice when you're at a party.

Hugh Downs told me a funny story on this point about a woman who interrupted a doctor and a lawyer who were chatting at a party to ask the doctor what she should do about a sore knee. He told her in some detail about hot compresses, cold compresses, keeping the knee elevated, and some pain-killing tablets to take.

After the woman left, the doctor looked at the lawyer in exasperation. "I think I should send her a bill, don't you?" he asked, and the lawyer replied, "Yes, you should." So the next day the doctor sent the woman a bill and the lawyer sent the doctor a bill.

The subtle approach is equally offensive and not so subtle at that. Women often are guilty of telling psychiatrists anecdotes about their children or husbands, fishing for some free professional insight, and men ramble on to lawyers about their problems with a hostile partner. This is really no different than asking a merchant that you've met to send you a free television set. Professionals sell a commodity too: their counsel; respect their right to save it for business hours.

This doesn't mean that you can't discuss his profession at all. If you're really interested in the subject, you can ask a doctor his attitude about the newest vaccines, for instance; or a psychiatrist if he thinks Freud is becoming obsolete; or a lawyer what judges can do when the defendants become unruly; or an architect if buildings change the people who use them. Don't waste his time if you haven't anything to contribute except the showpiece question; ask something that really intrigues you because you're sincerely interested and have some ideas of your own.

If the technicalities of his profession have no allure,

ask him instead if the preparation for his specialty has changed in recent years, what kind of young people are being attracted to his field, whether he would go into it today if he was starting over again, what are the drawbacks to a job that seems so impressive to outsiders.

And remember, especially with a doctor, that he is also a flesh and blood person. Just for a change, you might ask about *his* health.

3

how to talk to...
Royalty, and Other VIPs

When Prince Philip arrived for his unprecedented interview with me on that November morning in 1969, he was in a black mood. Unlike his wife, Queen Elizabeth II, he does not hold the view that royalty has an obligation to hide its displeasure; he's all man, he has a temper, and he shows it.

The NBC television camera crew and I had been waiting for him in the Presidential Suite of the Waldorf Towers (which incidentally is seedier than it sounds) and I was fairly sure I knew why the Prince was upset. As I pictured it, he had wakened a short time before feeling marvelous, thinking that his exhausting visit to the United States was over and he had only to drive to the airport, climb behind the controls of his plane and fly home to London.

At that point, as I imagined the scene, an aide would reluctantly remind him that late the night before he somehow had promised that a woman could interview him for a television show. The Prince then would have cried *Good grief*, or whatever Princes say in such circumstances, and stomped around wondering how he could ever have agreed to such madness. When I met him a few minutes later, he was wearing sports clothes, a tight expression, and looked taller and paler than I imagined him.

Actually I hadn't been the one who talked him into the interview—it was the President of the United States. On the previous afternoon I had been in the White House to do a television interview with Tricia Nixon and was fortunate to meet the President himself. I told him I had read that he was entertaining Prince Philip at an all-male dinner that evening. "This," I told him, teasingly, "is a classic example of discrimination against women."

The President was amused and said Washington wives had been in a flurry over it, adding that I surely would have ample opportunity to talk to the Prince when he appeared on the *Today* show. I told him that our invitation had been refused with an explanation that His Royal Highness was appearing on only one show during his visit, and that one was *Meet the Press*. President Nixon said that he was really sorry to hear that for he felt the relaxed interviews of *Today* would suit the Prince very well. He urged me to try again now at the British Embassy and he offered to mention it to the Prince himself later that night.

The Embassy politely said again that it was impossible, especially since the Prince was planning to return to England early the next morning. But never underestimate the power of a President. That night, an hour or so after midnight, the British Embassy telephoned me in New York to say that the Prince had agreed to the interview after all and would meet me in his Waldorf suite just before he was to fly home. I hurriedly asked how to address him correctly, which I consider imperative preparation for meeting a dignitary, and was informed that Your Royal Highness, Prince Philip, or *Sir* were all acceptable, but *Duke* was definitely out. I inquired if there was some special subject that the Prince wanted to discuss and was told to ask him.

So there I was the next morning, uneasily facing one of the most formidable interviews of my career and fully sympathetic with the Prince's grouchiness, though it didn't help my butterflies. He was criticizing everything: the lights, the chair he was to sit in, the cameras, *everything*. I asked if there were a topic in particular that he would like me to introduce, and he replied curtly, "No." Somewhat rattled, I tried to put him in a better mood by telling him that I had reported on that summer's investiture of his son as Prince of Wales, and that Americans had so much enjoyed the historical pageant on television. He looked at me levelly and said, "Can't we get on with this?"

We could and the film began to roll, I began with a question suggested by President Nixon. He had told me about a poll in Great Britain which reported that if citizens there were to elect a president, they would choose Prince Philip. It seemed a promising place to start because I could mention President Nixon's interest and indirectly compliment the Prince on his popularity at the same time. So I said all that in a brief preamble and asked Prince Philip if he would have enjoyed being a politician. He responded without warmth that this was a hypothetical question, which he didn't normally answer.

I was crushed, but I learned a valuable lesson about talking to people in very high places, which I hereby pass along to you: avoid the hypothetical question, of the sort that usually begins "What if . . ." and then departs into some fanciful situation that never happened and never will. That type of question can be asked of creative people, for whom imaginary situations are intriguing, but practical, crisp people dismiss it as a waste of time.

With Prince Philip I promptly switched to direct questions about personal concerns and was rewarded with one of the best interviews I've ever had. I asked him, for instance, if he felt frustrated that his outspokenness sometimes caused a storm of reaction, to which he replied that it was preferable to a life of "bromides and platitudes," and what he thought of parental permissiveness (against it), and, tactfully, if the monarchy is out of date (not yet), and if royal children are idle (they're not).

There was an unexpectedly candid reply to a question I was trying to put delicately about his secondary status in relationship to his wife. "Your Highness," I asked, "you are so much your own man that I wonder if during the early years of your marriage you found it . . ." As I searched for the diplomatic word, he laughed and said, "It was difficult, yes . . . Inevitably it's an awkward situation to be in."

"But," I went on, "do you get used to it?" With a smile the Prince replied, "Oh, you get used to anything. You'd be surprised."

The question that led to all the headlines in British newspapers concerned the possibility that the Queen might some day abdicate and turn the throne over to her son so that he could have the opportunity to rule while still a young man. Prince Philip commented that there was little chance of that, "But," he added, "who can tell? Anything might happen."

The United States press considered this answer inconsequential, but the British newspapers were electrified with the statement that gave any hint that such a possibility might ever take place. To calm the uproar, Buckingham Palace had to issue a special communiqué stating that the Queen had no intention of abdicating. I wrote the Prince a note expressing my distress that the interview had caused him embarrassment and received back a charming letter from him on imposing Buckingham Palace stationery. He thanked me for my concern and explained that I wasn't to worry, the initial reaction had been based on hearsay and evaporated as soon as the real facts were known. He added an ascerbic dig at journalists whom he described as too busy to read a discussion or speech before commentating on it.

He signed the letter simply, "Philip," which is the royal way—the Queen signs hers "Elizabeth." Just the same, I'm thinking of writing him again and signing my letter "Babs."

I learned from this encounter with one of the most royal personages on earth that my rules for conversation are reliable even in the most adverse circumstances. Except for the mistake about the hypothetical question, which I won't make again, I had asked him about matters that affected him personally, and he had wanted to reply to them.

I used the same approach when I talked with Princess Grace of Monaco. As with many professional performers, she was acutely uncomfortable to be in front of cameras without a script and, I am told, confided in friends that she didn't believe she had done very well. I disagree. I think few people who saw that interview will ever forget her answer when I asked if she was fulfilled in her life as a princess. She said, "I have a certain peace of mind."

Royalty, however, and even semi-royalty, is a comparatively rare species. The VIPs most of us encounter from time to time are more likely to be diplomats, politicians, the military, or clergy. With any of these, the best response follows a human approach, which is what this book is all about. Treat them as people who suffer the same amount of fatigue, joy, disillusionment, and boredom as anyone else. They are not figureheads or spokesmen, but living beings with feelings like your own—it's your meeting ground.

If you ask ponderous questions designed to demonstrate your penetrating intellect, you're likely to get a glib reply that the VIP has delivered from a podium a hundred times.

But there are some differences in talking to these various categories of VIP, and one group must be handled with all the care and strategy that you would accord an undetonated bomb you happened to find in the petunias.

I mean politicians. It used to be said that there were three topics that couldn't be discussed in polite company: politics, religion, and sex. In recent years, religion has become one of the most stimulating and safe subjects for conversation around, and sex is talked about so often that it's almost routine.

This leaves politics, which only a few years ago would have put any party to sleep. Today it is the hottest, most dangerous subject in the land. It's not only a conversation-wrecker, it's a friendship-wrecker, a family-wrecker, a job-wrecker, a future-wrecker. If we could harness the destructive energy of disagreements over politics, we wouldn't need the bomb.

The next few paragraphs, therefore, will not deal only with How to Talk with a Politician; anyone can do *that* at the drop of a gauntlet. Instead we will discuss How to Talk with a Politician *Without Arguing*, which is vastly more difficult.

The first rule is to take your own temperature. If you are violently opposed to all his views, if the very sight of him across the room causes your blood pressure to rise, know thyself and keep your distance. It's not likely you can get through even the civilities of the introduction without growing flushed and insensate, so stay away from him entirely. If you're really seething, you'd better get your coat and go.

Please understand that I'm not advocating avoidance of confrontation as your life style—blandness isn't interesting or desirable in an individual or in a nation. Maybe you'd rather act on the pure but doubtful hope that you can convert him with ringing truths and that when you're finished he'll be grateful that you put him on the right track at last. Perhaps you'll decide that you simply have to tell him off, for the sake of your integrity and blood pressure. If you must, go ahead—but that's for another book, maybe one about revolution. This book is about friendly, civil, enjoyable conversation.

I'm afraid that what is happening in this age of radicalizing opinions is that we are beginning to cancel one another out on the basis of our political beliefs. If the other person's convictions coincide with ours, he's an all-round great guy. If not, then his good humor, his tenderness with his crippled mother and his support of the symphony count for nothing.

The *Today* program, because it is allied with the news department, is obliged to be as neutral as possible. As a result, no one really knows what our point of view is on major issues. Conservatives write and tell us we are radicals, radicals write that we are conservative. Because of my efforts to at least appear objective, I can truthfully see two sides to almost any issue. This doesn't stop me from forming a personal opinion, but it does stop me from feeling that anyone who doesn't agree with me is full of malarkey.

If you've watched many interview programs in which political figures or controversial persons in general are being questioned, you'll have noticed a technique which we use often on *Today* and which will work just as well in your living room. Instead of saying, "You're nuts," or "You're absolutely wrong, that bill was passed in 1962 and had nothing to do with integration," you play the Devil's Advocate in the third person or persons. Start out, "There are those who say," or even better, "Some observers say" and then make your statement. It makes the attack less personal and you are no longer the antagonist but rather someone with background knowledge who is just repeating what he has heard.

Newsmen do this so they will not appear biased or personal. Listen one evening to the commentators and see how often you hear phrases like, "Observers say"—"An informed source reports"—"There are those who feel"—If it's good enough for Eric Sevareid, it's good enough for you.

Now then, if all this fails, if you don't think you can talk politics with him without getting emotional, or if you've met the politician at a private party and you think he would prefer being off duty, stick to the questions in other areas that will make him comfortable and give you some points to contribute.

Ask him how he handles the risk of disappointment when campaigning for office—we've all wanted something desperately, but only the daring or the tough try for it so publicly. Ask him about the pressure on his family to be model people because all eyes are on them. Ask him if he was a leader when he was a small boy. Ask him what taught him the most about succeeding in life. Ask him if politicians with opposite views ever become close friends. Ask him if he feels an obligation to be trim, neat, and barbered at all times. Ask him if he can manage the time to have a hobby. Ask if he has a hero.

I once had a surprisingly informal chat with Lyndon Johnson, during the time he was President, and it resulted from this kind of personal interest question. It happened when I was in the White House one day preparing a story on Mrs. Johnson. Her much respected press secretary, Liz Carpenter, received a message from the President saying that he would like to have me drop by.

I was surprised and flattered, and was mumbling to Liz Carpenter all the way down the corridor, that I certainly hadn't expected such a meeting when I found myself abruptly in the large oval office, where President Johnson was sitting in a rocking chair facing a portrait of Franklin D. Roosevelt. (By the way, now in President Nixon's office, that portrait has been replaced by one of Dwight D. Eisenhower.) I sat down on a red couch next to President Johnson's chair and he asked if I would like a Fresca. At the time, I'd never heard of this soft drink and thought wildly that it might be the name of a new dance, but I said yes anyway—and went on wondering what to say next.

Think human, I told myself, and remembered that this was the day of the President's thirty-third wedding anniversary, so I asked, "Mr. President, your relationship with your wife is something that even Republicans can only admire. I have just been married for five years. Truthfully, in your opinion what makes a good marriage?" The President then gave me a long personal account of his marriage to Lady Bird, and how well she had raised the children despite his frequent absences, especially when they were young, and what a helpmate she had been all their married lives.

Our conversation had been so disarmingly friendly that I felt courageous enough when it ended to say, "Mr. President, do you suppose a reporter can ask to kiss a President? Because," I continued, "it's your anniversary and I've had such a splendid time, I'd like to kiss you on the cheek." The President raised his eyebrows and gave me an injured grin. "Barbara," he said, "that's like those unpleasant bills in Congress. I like the motion, but I don't like the rules."

I had no time for preparation before meeting President Johnson, but I knew that the correct form of addressing him was either "Mr. President" or "Sir." If you have a chance before meeting any VIP in political life, find out the correct way to address him. You can get the information simply by telephoning his secretary or by discreetly asking someone who accompanies him, or by checking in some reference book. I rely on one that belongs to my secretary. It's titled *Communications, Handbook for Secretaries*, by Lucy Graves Mayo, and it contains a chapter setting out the proper salutations for dignitaries. A member of the cabinet, for instance, is called Mr. Secretary or Madam Secretary, a U.S. ambassador is Mr. Ambassador or Madam Ambassador, foreign ambassadors are Mr. Ambassador, Madam Ambassador, or Your Excellency, archbishops in the United States are Most Reverend Sir, Your Excellency or Archbishop. If you are presented to the Pope, he is called Your Holiness.

If you care about giving the impression that you're a tactful, considerate, and resourceful person, it's essential that you take the trouble to get this kind of information. If the person is in office, it isn't difficult to get it right— but you may be in trouble when the man no longer holds his high position. Strictly speaking, he's plain "mister" again but, human nature being what it is, he still likes the majestic sound of that title.

It operates according to an unwritten law of its own: the more lofty the title, the more likely it is that the man will cling to it for the rest of his days. Corporals are willing to forget their rank instantly upon discharge, majors sometimes, generals never. (Former President Eisenhower, for instance, requested that he be buried in full military uniform.) Joseph P. Kennedy liked to be called "Mr. Ambassador" throughout the thirty years that he lived after leaving the Court of St. James's. By law, U.S. Presidents keep their title after they leave the White House, and are known as Mr. President until the end of their days. Judges feel the same attachment to their title, and so do most senators and congressmen and members of cabinet. I interviewed Dean Rusk two months after he left the office of Secretary of State, and referred to him as Mr. Secretary throughout.

Sometimes a very distinguished career politician will hold several important posts during his lifetime. When in doubt, it is wise to use the most imposing title in the selection, but this doesn't always work. Averell Harriman, for instance, liked to be called Governor even after he had been an ambassador.

Please note, as well, that college deans and professors, most high ranking scientists and some clergymen hold

49

doctorate degrees in their specialties. Protocol is tenderly careful not to demote them by calling them Mister—their livelihoods are sometimes dependent upon their more prestigious title. You should follow this example, even at the risk of confusing the sizable group of people who think all doctors should be able to explain a skin rash. If you aren't sure, ask in the more flattering manner of "Dr. Pusey, do you prefer that we call you Doctor or Mister?" rather than, "Mr. Pusey, would you prefer that we call you Doctor or Mister?"

As I write this, I can't help but remember the late James Pike the last time I interviewed him. He had recently resigned as an Episcopalian bishop. "Do I call you Bishop or Mr. Pike?" I asked. He answered, "How about just 'Jim'?"

Getting the title right is important, particularly in the first impression stage of a conversation with a VIP, but so is being frank if you don't know much about the city or state or foreign country he represents. People readily forgive an honest declaration of ignorance—in fact, in these days of bluff and brittleness it will be viewed as downright charming.

There's nothing more flattering than true curiosity. "Tell me, Mayor, I know very little about your city, what are its most distinguishing features?"; "What are you proudest of in your city?"; "What is it famous for?"; "What is its leading industry?"

Or, "Ah! You're from Tanzania. I'm not sure what Tanzania was called before its independence." That's infinitely preferable to a dumb stab in the dark like, "Oh yes, Tanzania—that was the Congo before its independence."

Mrs. Spiro Agnew appeared on the *Today* program just after returning from her trip with the Vice-President to the teeming countries of the Far East. It was the first time she had ever left the United States and I was curious to discover how she had survived the culture shock. It was no problem at all, she told me; she got along with greeting dignitaries by asking about the buildings and schools and shrines. And she didn't pretend that she knew it all already.

Like politicians, diplomats today can arouse passionate controversy. If you feel a strong necessity to lay down a verbal assault against the man from an Arab country, for instance, or South Africa or Hungary, go right ahead. But you won't be accomplishing anything because you can't possibly change his mind, and you'll have missed an opportunity to gain an insight into his thinking. I would advise keeping away from him if you can't be polite.

Happily most diplomats come from countries that don't provoke instant hostility; in general, they are a witty, and sophisticated group of people. I have particular fondness for Lord Hugh Caradon, the British Ambassador to the United Nations. I met him at a dinner party, where I was delighted to be seated next to him. But when I thought of starting a conversation with him, I felt overwhelmed—at that time Lord Caradon was in the midst of two controversies, one a settlement of a dispute between his own country and the small island of Anguilla, and the other his role as one of the representatives to the Big Four conference on the Middle East crisis.

Because, like most Americans, I was concerned with the crisis in the Middle East, I asked Lord Caradon first for his own analysis of the situation. It was a rare privilege for me to hear his views. But I knew little about Anguilla, and I didn't want Lord Caradon to feel that he had to conduct a seminar over the roast beef. Besides, I was curious about other more personal aspects of his life. So I said, "In dealing with heads of state and other diplomats, how do you know if you're getting through or if they're just being diplomatically polite?"

Lord Caradon couldn't have been more pleased by the question. He illustrated his answer by telling me about an issue before the United Nations which had recently come to a vote. A high ranking member of the Soviet mission had assured him that the Soviets would support the British position. Lord Caradon told me that he knew and instinctively trusted the Soviet diplomat; his advisers in Great Britain, however, were skeptical and warned him not to have faith in the Soviet promise. But when the issue was put to the vote, the Soviets did go along with the British— Lord Caradon had never doubted that they would.

When it came time to talk of other things, I asked Lord Caradon if he was required to attend such dinner parties every week, and what he did in an average day, the sorts of questions that interested me and gave Lord Caradon an opportunity to talk about himself as a person, rather than a walking Union Jack.

Diplomats are marvelous conversationalists, as you might expect, but nowadays so are clergymen. We're finding on the *Today* show that clergymen are among our most articulate, attractive guests, but I can remember a time when people dreaded being stuck in a conversation with a clergyman because it seemed certain to be pompous and dreary.

All that changed about a decade ago when the Rt. Rev. James Robinson, English Bishop of Woolwich, declared that God was dead and Pope John XXIII announced that he intended to "open a window." There's almost *nothing* you can't talk about to a clergyman. Except for the fundamentalists, whose beliefs must be accorded courteous respect (the possibility of a fast liberalizing during the salad course is remote anyway), most clergymen today seem to be ready to discuss religion in flexible, non-defensive, and even startling terms. And a great many of them know more about their community's poverty, racial, and mental health problems than the politicians or social workers.

So feel free to ask questions that you might not have a few years ago. Ask him about the changes in his church. You can ask a priest how he feels about the pill, or abortion, or marriage for priests and nuns. If you're a church or temple goer, mention what is happening in your congregation that's unusual, and ask him if there's something similar happening in his. Ask about his involvement in secular matters. Does he feel the church belongs on the street? Ask him what led him to decide to devote his life to religion, and, if you're getting along swimmingly, you can even dare to ask what holds him and if he sometimes considers leaving the pulpit.

I asked such a question of Bishop James Pike, just before he set off for Israel and met his tragic death. I commented that he had officially left his church and he was showing a great interest in the Old Testament and Hebraic scholarship. What would separate him from becoming a rabbi in the future? He answered that, indeed, he didn't see much separation, actually, but he was now still a Christian.

Switching to a different topic, a rabbi I know tells me that one of the hazards of his calling is the lonely female member of the congregation who sees her pastor as the

53

most desirable man in the world. It's a well-known phenomenon; lecturers at theological colleges warn about it. If you've established a comfortable relationship with the clergyman, you can ask about that.

The final category I've arbitrarily included among the VIPs is the military and I can't emphasize too strongly that it is unfair, and perhaps even malicious, to challenge him with statements about war being unhealthy for children and other living things. He has dedicated his life, and is ready to sacrifice that life, to the conviction that if the government is tyrannical, peace can also be unhealthy for children and other living things. Find some neutral ground for conversation or don't talk to him at all.

This lesson was reinforced for me when I was at a small dinner party in West Berlin. The *Today* show was broadcasting a week of programs from West Germany and I was introduced to Major General Robert G. Ferguson and told that he was the U. S. Commandant in the city. The thought of asking him how he felt about the Vietnam War flitted across my mind, but I decided against it and instead asked him what our forces did in Germany and how they educated their children, and if living in Europe changed them.

I'm so grateful that I didn't mention Vietnam: I learned later that the general's son had been killed there.

If he is a career sailor, marine, or soldier, ask him instead how he happened to choose that way of life. Ask him if he sometimes feels constricted and would like to get out. Ask him how the military has changed since he started in it.

And don't make the mistake of thinking that he has no interest except the military—I've noticed that many officers have unusual hobbies and I'm intrigued that these often are gentle pastimes such as gardening and bird-watching.

If the man saw action, you might, with tact, ask him about that; men sometimes want to relive the war. When I interviewed the *Pueblo* captain, Commander Lloyd M. Bucher, I wondered if he would cringe from recounting the details of his imprisonment in North Korea but I found just the reverse—he urgently wanted me and the audience to know what it had been like. I think he will be talking about his year as a prisoner for the rest of his life. Talking about it perhaps helps him to endure it.

If the military you've just met happens to be a serviceman fresh from Vietnam, feel him out before you rush in with questions about battle. Most veterans like to talk about their lives under fire, but there are a few whose agony is so intense they can't trust themselves to describe the war at all. If you sense such reluctance, find another subject instantly, one related to his civilian life.

In general, tread very lightly; perhaps it's best to find out from someone who knows him how traumatic the war was for him, before you touch the topic at all. But if he is eager to recall his days in Vietnam, have the decency not to bait him with questions about massacres and black markets. And don't tell him all the things you know that he doesn't. He saw his friends shipped home in boxes, and he's earned the right to believe that it counted for something.

Keep the discussion generalized. Ask him what life is like in the cities of Vietnam, as opposed to the rural areas. Ask if his attitude changed while he was away. Ask him about the commuter aspect of the war, that men were delivered to the battle every morning and returned to base at night—was that easier on the nerves than sustained fighting, or worse? Ask, if the medical side of war interests you, about the quickness of aid for the wounded. Ask (everyone does) about the availability of marijuana. Ask about the heat, the dampness, the housing.

If, however, he wants to know *your* opinion of the Vietnam War, everything is fair. Don't harangue, and don't make it a personal attack on him, and try to be brief. But you are entitled to unburden yourself of your feelings, when asked.

SPECIAL CIRCUMSTANCES

The Wives: The women who marry VIPs get accustomed to thinking of themselves as part of the background because their dazzling husbands attract almost all the available attention. But it's a mistake to be taken in by their deliberate self-effacement. In the first place, these women have interesting, unusual lives and have had to develop an abnormal amount of resourcefulness in order to cope with the unexpected. All of which means you can learn a lot and simultaneously be entertained by asking them how they manage their households.

Mamie Eisenhower, for instance, told me on television that her greatest difficulty in the White House years was managing three sets of servants—the White House has to be staffed around the clock. She also wanted it known that she and President Eisenhower paid all their personal expenses out of their own pocket while in office. "Maybe other Presidents don't do that," she said with spirit, "but it was our way." And she reflected that perhaps she had the easiest time adjusting to the White House of any presidential wife, because she was so accustomed to moving. "I bring along some Oriental rugs and some pictures," she smiled, "and it's home."

Mary Lindsay, wife of New York City's mayor, told me that her biggest headache in living in the city-owned Gracie Mansion, was keeping the rugs from falling apart. At campaign time, thousands of people tramped over them.

A considerable number of VIP wives have the kinds of personalities that make them every bit as stimulating company as their husbands. I'm thinking in particular of Marian Javits, wife of the senior Republican Senator from New York, who flatly refuses to play her assigned role of indistinct, indistinguishable woman. Many politicians' wives tend to be cautious, holding no opinions in public stronger than the sanctity of motherhood, but Mrs. Javits is emphatically of another breed altogether.

She's noted as a maverick, who openly admits to five and a half years of psychoanalysis to "distill and clarify" her personality. During the time when her husband was rumored to be a possible candidate for the vice-presidency, when it might have been assumed that she would be especially guarded with reporters, she gave me an interview in which she declared that she disliked Washington and would never live there, regretted that the Kennedy Center was located in what she described as a culturally empty city, detested cocktail parties and believed that many Senate wives neglected their children. And that was only the first five minutes of the interview.

I recently interviewed the wives of five members of President Nixon's cabinet and found them involved and excit-

57

ing women on their own. And for adding spice and color to any gathering, one need go no further than talk with the most controversial of the Washington wives, Martha Mitchell.

Clergymen's wives, like their husbands, are also likely to be more vivid and gregarious than that shy, wan stereotype of some years back. Instead of pouring tea from a silver service for a group of ladies in hats, they are more likely today to spend their afternoons in a drop-in center for lonely kids, sipping coffee with them from chipped mugs. And even more likely, they may be upgrading their education, or holding full-time jobs.

You can talk to them about their community activity, and if they feel an obligation to go around spreading kindness and sunshine because of their husband's vocation. Ask them if people's expectations about the character of the pastor's wife have changed in recent years, if they feel more freedom now. Ask if they were concerned to be marrying a man who planned to devote his life to religion. Ask if raising children in the shadow of the pulpit presents any difficulties of its own. Ask if she and her husband agree on religious matters.

These questions can be adapted to fit any VIP wife, but especially one who is married to a military man. She lives in a community of her own, barricaded visibly and invisibly from civilian society. Ask her about her life, her adjustment to impermanence, her feelings about raising children in a military environment, and about the social life on a base.

Never underestimate the ladies; you can miss a great conversation that way.

4

how to talk to... *The Young and the Old*

You're talking across a gap, but it's only years. Whether you're confronted by a seventy-year-old lady with that expression of hesitant humbleness that some use so effectively, or a fifteen-year-old youth with flat eyes and no expression at all, you're still dealing with a person who, like you, hates to be patronized, hopes to be able to be genuine, and is depressed by the thought of being disliked.

You have more in common with either than you think. All generations have concerns about pollution and computerized society; all generations waken in the dark middle of the night and feel loneliness; all generations respond to spring, friendships, and courage. Don't think it's hopeless to attempt a conversation just because you can't remember Calvin Coolidge or never say *outasight*. Wade in, anticipating an interesting time, and the water will be warm.

But be prepared to listen. The barriers between the generations aren't caused by a failure to talk to one another: they're talking all the time, but no one listens.

From dozens of interviews with teenagers I offer these

cautions to avoid getting off on the wrong foot. The first is not to assume that all teenagers are alike; they aren't, any more than all forty-year-olds are alike. So don't begin with "You teenagers seem to feel . . ." or, "All young people nowadays . . ."

And don't ask right off the bat about drugs, because adults *always* ask teenagers about drugs and they are fed up with the question and the hostility they sense behind it. And they're even fed up with their own stock answers whether it's, "I really don't know. I've never tried them and neither have any of my friends," or, "It's something like alcohol use, you drink don't you?" or, venomously, "I understand tranquilizers are becoming a serious problem with you adults." As you can see, the conversation is going nowhere.

If you have a fairly private place to talk, and if you're giving the impression of being a reasonable person, the subject of drugs may arise naturally. They are very much on the mind of youth today, and adults who don't assume a fighting stance at the mention of the word marijuana are rare in the world. He'll be grateful to have met you.

And don't make the common error of measuring drug consumption by length of hair. Young people take derisive enjoyment from the fact that the long-haired kids their parents won't have in the house may not be drug-users at all, while the scrubbed, brush-cut neighbor in the three-piece suit, widely admired as a model boy, may be the biggest pusher in the school.

Further, you don't have to talk their language or dress like a hippie in order to communicate with young people. We have enough young people—what we need is more adults. As Steve Lawrence, a very funny man as well as a fine singer, put it, "The only problem I find with the generation gap is that it isn't wide enough."

There's one final *don't*: don't ask young people about the sexual revolution. There's a distasteful element of voyeurism and envy in such questions, and, besides, it is none of your business. As the sixteen-year-old daughter of a friend of mine remarked crisply, "After all, we don't ask our parents' friends, 'How's the wife-swapping coming along?' "

Be honest, that's really all that kids require. The shrill, cloying adults in the film *The Graduate* are good examples of how not to behave. Be simple, be direct, be open. It's very difficult for adults not to do all the talking when holding a conversation with a young person. It's comfortable that way, of course, and both the adult and adolescent are accustomed to the one-way flow of wisdom and opinion. But if you try to reverse roles and put yourself in the pupil position, the effect is magic.

A middle-aged guest on our program told us of his encounter with a motorcycle gang one summer night. He had driven to an almost deserted shopping plaza to buy some cigarettes and came out of the drug store to find that a dozen young people in those sinister-looking leather jackets had pulled up on their motorcycles and were blocking his passage to his car.

He considered the situation, stalling for time by opening the cigarette package and going through his pockets for matches. They watched him, silent as cats. If he walked around them, he would look foolish and his ego would hurt; the alternative, walking through that still cluster of menace, was equally unacceptable. He acknowledged to himself that he was afraid.

"I've often wondered," he said, in what he hoped was a normal tone of voice, "why you have those high handle-bars. Is there some advantage in them?" The bikers, he later reported, nearly fell over themselves answering him. They demonstrated how small a circle they could turn, how maneuverable they were, and some safety factors. He was amazed at how much they knew about motor-cycle design and engineering.

In the end, when he moved toward his car, they pulled back to give him room and called goodbye to him until he had driven away.

An excellent small book by a child psychiatrist, Dr. John Rich, gives tips on techniques for talking to young people. Called *Interviewing Children and Adolescents*, it is intended for use by professionals in teaching and child therapy but it is very helpful to any adult who feels awk-ward with adolescents.

"It is not so much interests and preferences that are important," Dr. Rich writes, "as an attitude toward life. If the child says that he loves milk chocolate and the adult says that he personally prefers olives, they are still on com-mon ground because the adult can get as enthusiastic about olives as the child can about chocolate."

It's a good observation. If you're very responsive to Beethoven, tell the teenager something of how you feel and ask what emotions his favorite music provokes in him. Ask him why volume is so important to music listen-ing among young people. If you go to movies, ask him what he looks for in a movie, does he go to be part of a fantasy or to recognize himself.

Ask him about his heroes. Is John Kennedy a hero today? Abbie Hoffman? Ask him about the credibility of newspapers—does he believe his hometown paper, an underground paper, television commentators? Ask him what changes are taking place in his high school, and if they make him uneasy, or impatient. Ask about anything currently in the news; and then *listen*. If you're talking to a teenaged girl, these questions fit her as well. Or you can ask her about the straight-hair, clean-face look of most young girls. Do her friends wear make-up at all, except for the eyes? Ask her how she feels about the women's liberation movement, and if she thinks marriage is going out of style. Ask her if she would describe herself as romantic or realistic, and if she believes there is a change in the fundamental nature of young people today, as compared with previous generations. Margaret Mead recently described them as a generation without precedent in the human race. Would she agree? Does she think her friends are under a great deal of stress?

We've asked questions like these of the teenagers who have been guests on the *Today* program, and we're impressed at their thoughtful and articulate answers. Perhaps we're seeing an elite group who aren't representative of young people on the whole, but I'm inclined to believe that they aren't unusual at all. I think any adult who shows respect and interest can have a relaxed and informative conversation with a teenager.

I presume you won't make the irretrievable mistake of describing how things were in your day, and how much tougher it was to be young, and how much more energy, courtesy and moral fibre you and your friends demonstrated then. Plato had the same complaint about the younger generation of his day—he thought permissive parents were the root of the problem. I'm sure they reacted as young people have ever since: they went stone deaf, waited until his lips stopped moving, and then fled.

Haim Ginott, the child psychologist who is familiar to *Today* audiences, has another good suggestion for adults. He advises us not to scoff or ridicule when young people tell of their problems, particularly those poignant ones about a first love that some of us tend to find sweet and amusing. They weren't funny when we were fourteen; remember that. When a young person grieves, tell him with sympathy, "I know, I know; it hurts." You'll find compassion, rather than adult logic or cynicism, will make him open up to you.

But this doesn't mean that you have to be unctuous and agreeable even when the teenager is tramping on your most treasured beliefs. Don't preach, don't get excited, but tell him or her what you hold to be true about the human condition. Fuzzy, indecisive adults are useless to the adolescent trying to sort himself out by testing his ideas against those of others.

After all, you're just as entitled to express yourself as he is. Not *more* entitled—it's unscrupulous to pull rank during a debate—but just as entitled.

Similarly, I hold that adults should be firm about the standards they require of young people under their roof, related or not. If you don't approve of their drinking, don't be a good fellow and allow it. If you want them back at a certain time, for dinner or curfew, consult with them to establish what is reasonable and then make it clear that they must observe it. If teenaged girls are visiting you, make certain that their parents know where they are; if your own teenagers are going somewhere, don't hesitate to find out where it is and who'll be there.

And don't apologize for playing the heavy. As Art Buchwald once observed, what kid wants a forty-year-old for a pal anyway.

Sometimes your encounter with a teenager is obviously going to be so brief that an extended conversation is out of the question. This happens if it's a young daughter who is helping to serve at her parents' cocktail party, or when you've met an old friend on the street and he introduces you to the son he has in tow. In such circumstances, I've known normally witty adults who plunge abruptly into an imitation of everyone's silly aunt. They'll squeak, "My, how you've grown!" or, "You look exactly like your mother, it's amazing!" or, "Imagine this being your son, I can't believe it!"—what is *that* supposed to mean?

You don't have to communicate with every young person you meet, and you don't have to nail down the title of Miss Ingratiating Personality right that minute. Just say, "How do you do," or, "It's nice to meet you," and let it go at that. Dignity is a classy commodity.

There's one other touchy situation which can crop up when mingling with the young. I'm talking about the growing number of young people in their late teens and early twenties who have established residence together without picking up a marriage license en route. Even liberal-minded adults are sometimes flustered by them, perhaps not so much by what they are doing—which is by no means unique in history—as by their openness about it.

How, for instance, do you introduce such a couple? They are not "engaged"; "common-law" is grotesque; "roommates" is flippant; "living in sin" is ridiculous. Until our language produces a better term, introduce them as "our daughter Jean, and her friend Bill Forbes." That's all anyone needs to know, unless the couple wants to make their relationship apparent by discussing their recent trip to Mexico or their problems with their landlord.

If you are still shocked when meeting such a couple, keep it to yourself. Try to talk to them naturally as you would any other pair, keeping to impersonal topics such as their reaction to the latest congressional investigation, or the new soup-can art show at the downtown gallery. If you can't trust yourself to control your moral indignation, exchange some brief pleasantries about the party or the weather and move along to talk to someone else.

Some adults can't imagine that it could ever be rewarding to talk to *any* young people, living together or not. Most particularly, they discount the possibility that a child not yet in his teens could have anything of interest to say except goodbye. Teenagers disturb them in prickly ways they don't want to analyze, but younger children make no impression at all.

As it happens they don't often have an opportunity to find out otherwise, and I wouldn't want to disturb that situation. Parents of young children should realize that few people, and maybe no one, will find their children as enchanting as they do. I much admire the attitude of a friend of my mother's who, when she came to visit, used to fix ten-year-old me with a hard look and say imperiously, "I came to talk to your mother. You can go."

I may have felt wounded at the time but I applaud her now. I don't care for children lingering in the room when adults are talking. I shudder as some wide-eyed eight-year-old watches unblinking as adults drink a little too much, flirt a little too much, and criticize absent friends a lot too much. And I don't find it adorable when she laughs in the right place at a dirty joke.

But there are times when the child must remain in the room with adults. When this happens, and you're faced with more than five minutes in the company of a young child, don't ask about school. As Dr. Rich comments in his book about interviewing children, adults would never think of opening a conversation with another adult by asking, "Are you successful in your job?"

He recommends asking questions in concrete form. Rather than inquiring if the child has any hobbies, a term he may not understand, ask rather what he likes to do after school. Ask a little girl if she picks out her own clothes. Ask younger children to show you their favorite toy or tell you their favorite story or name their favorite friend and tell you why they like the friend so much. Ask them what things scare them—children have interesting fears.

Very young children, my toddler for instance, are absolutely bowled over by a sparkling game of peek-a-boo. And infants are beguiled by keys on a chain. (This book isn't called *How to Talk with Practically Anybody About Practically Anything* for nothing.)

If you want something really exotic in the way of a conversation with a child, ask a philosophical question. I know a family who invited a powerhouse career girl to dinner and allowed their seven-year-old daughter to join them. The guest opened the conversation briskly by asking, "Well, Jill, what do you think God is?" Jill, as it turned out, had a number of concepts about God, all of them news to her dazed parents.

Even small children today have thoughts about poverty,

67

prisons, war, and what's fair, a synthesis of what they've overheard adults say and what they've seen on television, screened through their own considerable comprehension. You'll be amazed how much little boys know about space and the ideas little girls have about women's role in the world. I once polled a dozen kindergarten children for a special television film, asking them all "What do you think of the war in Vietnam?" The answer I liked most came from a four-year-old tot, who said sadly, "I don't know— I go to bed early." To her, the war began and ended on the seven o'clock news.

By the way, trite as it is, most children still respond to the favorite adult gambit, "What do you want to be when you grow up?" Just don't lean on him—the sons of Charles Mayo, the third Mayo doctor in that distinguished line that founded the Mayo Clinic in Rochester, Minnesota, heard nothing but, "I suppose you're going to be a doctor when you grow up." Only one of the six of them did.

As for tiny children, I recommend that you just sit back and let them stare, disconcerting as it is. Don't pounce on them or try to hug and pick them up until they make the first move. If you want to expedite matters, get down low to the child's eye level, keep your voice soft and friendly, ask the child to bring you something.

And don't feel bad if it doesn't work, if the child refuses flatly to come near you. A two-year-old is not an infallible judge of character. My cousin once introduced his then tiny son to a friend and the little boy stared for a moment and then shouted, "I don't like you!" My cousin, thinking his friend would be embarrassed, said hastily, "I know he doesn't mean it." His friend shrugged, "What if he does?"

On the other end of the human spectrum are the old. Only a few old people are fortunate enough to arrive near the end of their days with their personalities intact, and to surmount their own infirmities with humor and a lively interest in current events. These gutsy and compelling people generally are the kind who have been enthusiasts all their lives, as in e.e. cummings' lovely tribute, "He wore his life like a sky."

They pose no problem for conversation because they remain contemporary. Their great gift to all who meet them is the perspective they can provide. In their youth, all males had long hair, most politicians were rascals, students rioted and broke up the furniture, children were drunk on the streets and wars were manipulated in board rooms. They've got built-in *déjà vue*, and they can be very reassuring to this jittery world.

We all know a few of these wonders. Alfred Lunt and Lynn Fontanne come to my mind right away. She's in her eighties, yet she is still interested in fashion and sews her own clothes, while he retains buoyant humor and outlook. Elder Statesman Averell Harriman is hard of hearing but he has no trouble understanding the problems of the modern world, and his mind is as young and flexible as any junior congressman's. Author Philip Wylie appeared on a recent *Today* show and spoke of his preoccupation with the pollution problem; though well on in years, he worries that the world he may not live to see is irreversibly poisoning itself.

At the risk of sounding proud and prejudiced, I include my father, Lou Walters, in this category. At seventy-four he seems to me younger in spirit than most forty-year-olds, perhaps because he views the world and the people in it with good will and humor.

Most old people, however, require some effort on your part. They are disheartened to be living in the ailing house of their bodies, to be limited physically and economically, to feel an encumbrance to others—guests who didn't have the good manners to leave when the party was over.

There are two approaches which they will find gratifying and stimulating, and also will provide you with an absorbing conversation. One is to ask their opinions of today's massive social and technical changes. Do they think we should return to the extended families, where two or three generations lived close together and helped to raise the children? What do they think about women's rights? the clothes young people wear? the emergence of four-letter words? children dropping out of school? young people drifting? lakes too polluted for swimming? human extermination? men on the moon?

The other area to explore is their memories. It's a trick that works: when people recall a time when they were happier and more articulate, they *become* happier and more articulate. Ask about the radio shows he used to love, about the first car he ever drove, about the silent movies and what was the first sound picture he ever saw. Ask him how children played when he was young, and what schoolrooms were like, and what he remembers of his grandparents. Ask him what President does he recall most vividly and which one he disliked the most. Ask him about his courting days and what was the protocol then. Ask about his very first job—it still works as a conversation starter.

If you're talking to a much older woman, ask her about

the corsets of her time, and if she had a flapper haircut, and what people used to cook for family dinners, and how little girls were trained to be dutiful, and what people thought of working women then, and what she wore when she was married, and what was the best party she ever gave.

Keep in mind that you're talking to a living person, not a national shrine. An overload of condescending praise and reverent attention will make the old people feel they are lacking only an arrangement of lilies to be perfectly ready for embalming. If you disagree with their views on current events, argue back with vigor. A friend of mine visits a ninety-one-year-old who was his insurance broker, and they roar insults at one another as they have all the years they've known one another. A teenager I know plays poker regularly with his grandfather and grumbles and complains throughout while the old man grins, and assures him that he'll improve with age.

Speaking of grandchildren, if you happen to have a tolerance for discussions about children you will open a sluice-gate by asking old people about their grandchildren. You'll discover that, as it happens, their grandchildren are a perfect joy to be with . . . and to talk about.

Hearing declines in most everyone with age—it's a normal occurrence—and old people may be getting deaf. You'll have to speak a little louder and more slowly, pronouncing the words distinctly, but you don't have to descend to a simple vocabulary or trivial comments. Maybe because of that old expression "deaf and dumb," which implied "deaf and stupid," people denigrate the intelligence of deaf people. Because it is a nuisance to communicate, they often ignore them altogether. It's why deafness is regarded by the handicapped as the worst affliction, worse than blindness, worse than being crippled.

Take time to visit with the hard-of-hearing when you encounter one. If you're lucky, he'll tell you about the day the banks failed, or John Barrymore's *Hamlet*. If you have a relative who is becoming deaf, tell your guests to speak up a little; it's no disgrace. On *Today*, when a guest such as Jimmy Stewart tells us frankly that he is a bit deaf, we not only take pains to speak more loudly and slowly but we find it helps to look directly at the guest while we talk.

There are, however, times when you can be exceedingly unlucky in conversations with old people. A number of the aged have preserved, intact, the raw bigotry of the age in which they were raised. With easy, mindless contempt, they use the ugly words that lacerated minorities two generations ago; they haven't adjusted their vocabularies or softened their attitudes in fifty years.

And they're not going to be able to change in the few minutes that you have together. No matter how shocked and angry you are by what you have just heard an old person say, *don't preach*. All those fine sentiments about the pain of racial discrimination and the dignity of man will be totally lost on the very old; you will only bewilder and hurt them to no purpose. Accept their prejudice without comment, as you do any other infirmity that accompanies age.

My worst encounter of this kind happened during a live *Today* television interview with a seemingly charming old Southern horse-breeder. He was telling me about an incident with a famous horse and explained casually that the "nigger" gave him the reins. I froze, but came quickly to the decision that I couldn't possibly educate him right there. I waited until we were finished and he had gone, and then I turned to the camera and apologized to the viewers who had been offended, explaining that the guest hadn't realized how some terms affect others.

Another time I was preparing to interview for *Today* the elderly wife of one of the country's most distinguished politicians. While we were getting settled, she made some comment which included, in a whisper, the word "darkies." I was dismayed, but said nothing. I once knew a family where the very old Jewish patriarch used to rage against the *goyim*. The family would sigh regretfully, and try to change the subject. They saw no point, and neither do I, in getting excited about it.

Unless you like lengthy conversations about illness, I advise you not to mention health, hospitals, or doctors to old people. Even asking the conventional, "How are you today?" risks bringing down a cascade of miseries, medical neglect and new symptoms. Old people invariably suffer erosion of their vital parts but dwelling on discomforts only serves to increase their anxiety, and increased anxiety increases pain. To some extent you are what you talk about: when you talk about being sick, you feel sicker.

So don't start the conversation with, "Your son tells me that you slipped last week . . ." Ask instead what he thinks of girls wearing pants suits to the office. Ask if today's movies are any more sexy and revealing than the old Jean Harlow films. Ask him to describe the worst storm he ever experienced, the best music he ever heard, the biggest crowd he ever saw.

Your next problem may be making a graceful escape. The aging process seems to strike first at the mechanism

73

which warns that we have been talking too much and the listener is growing restless. The signal isn't perfect at any age—drink, for instance, throws it right out of kilter—but it is almost non-existent in old people.

You don't have to prove your essential decency by being a martyr. Listen for as long as you are interested, and then a few minutes longer. Let him finish one whole story, no matter how it rambles, and then leave quickly. Don't be brusque in your going, and don't make up some transparent lie. Thank him warmly for the interesting talk, tell him you enjoyed your few minutes with him, and then move firmly to join another group or go out of the room. If neither of these moves is possible because you're on a plane or in some other static seating situation, say pleasantly that you must do some reading now, or you think you'll take a nap.

Don't be too hasty though. Old people have witnessed a lot of history that books can never record, and some of them have been adventurous and antic in their youth. I remember the 102-year-old woman guest on *Today*. Her principal regret, it turned out, was that she was now too old to drive her racing car.

5

how to talk to...
Difficult People

Even the most poised conversationalist can be undone by such social situations, as, for instance, (1): being trapped with a bore whose single topic is his family's motor trip to Yellowstone Park, complete with daily mileage and road conditions, or (2): the drunk who gets you into focus by closing one eye and bellowing, "You think you're pretty smart, don't you baby," or (3): the haggard lady whose husband has just moved out, leaving her with lurid accounts of his depravity, which she now feels are required listening as a proof of friendship.

I've drawn up some suggestions for the most commonly encountered problem people, but you'll discover that I'm not in favor of escape as a unilateral policy. There are painful, tedious people in abundance and some of them must be suffered kindly, maybe even until they run down and have nothing more to say. Things being what they are in the world today, we are more and more driven to depend on one another's sympathy and friendship in order to survive emotionally. Most suicides occur when a person feels totally alone.

Furthermore, warm, sustaining relationships become especially important during those periods when we are our least lovable. People bursting with good will and an abundance of mental health are charming company; their need for ego-boosting, however, is minimal. People sinking into self-pity and depression are dreary, but they can't get out of it by themselves. So every now and then, just sit there and listen, and listen, and listen. You're paying your membership dues in the human race.

THE NEWLY BEREAVED

I interviewed Mamie Eisenhower in Augusta, Georgia, not long after General Eisenhower had died. When I asked her what she wanted to talk about, Mrs. Eisenhower replied firmly, "The happy times." She was suffering from laryngitis at the time and was concerned that people would misunderstand and think that she was struggling to keep from crying. She didn't want that kind of sympathy, and I think this holds true for most newly bereaved people. There's a long period after a death when self-control is fragile. Pity smashes it flat and leaves the bereaved person feeling naked and mortified.

Ethel Kennedy is another valiant widow who comes to mind. During the long sad ride that took her husband's body from New York to Washington, she walked the entire length of the train often smiling and making jokes with the mourners. She had said that she didn't want people to have to grieve with her—she'd do that in private—and she meant it.

Shortly after that funeral I talked to Rose Kennedy on

Today. She had buried three sons and a daughter, and I asked her what gave her the courage to keep going. I'll never forget her answer. It was, "I refuse to be vanquished."

My friend Kitty Carlisle Hart, widow of the playwright-director Moss Hart, has the same indomitable spirit. When preparing this book I asked her what she liked best and least to have strangers say to her. She answered, "I hate questions on what it's like to be a widow. It implies pity, and I hate pity—self-pity or any other kind."

When meeting a friend for the first time after there has been a death close to him, it's appropriate to offer condolences. Keep it very brief and simple, just enough to express sorrow that it happened, and then ask a question that will allow the friend to keep his composure. It can be related to the death, but not to his feeling of loss. Ask if he plans to move, or if most of the family were able to attend the funeral, or if he plans to go away for a while.

If you can't think of something sufficiently neutral, talk of something else entirely. A friend of ours whose beloved brother had died met a mutual friend on the street the next day. She was close to tears and dreaded talking to him for fear of making a spectacle of herself, but it couldn't be avoided. He looked at her somberly for a moment and said, "It's a damn shame," and then briskly told her how he'd been able to figure out that zoning problem that had been bothering her. She couldn't digest a word he was saying, but she remembers that she listened in a haze of gratitude for his tact.

You're going to have to use your own tact to gauge whether this is what the grieving person wants or not. If you have privacy, and if the death was recent, it's more likely that the person will want to talk of nothing else, will *need* to talk of nothing else. There's a Hebrew proverb about "wearing out" grief—if you bottle it up, you'll never soften it. "Give sorrow words," said Shakespeare. "The grief that does not speak whispers the o'er-fraught heart and bids it break."

It astonishes people who haven't gone through a death experience close to them, but some of grieving is happy recollection. The Irish are masters of the hilarious wake, but it isn't their exclusive property. At one point during my long, two-part interview with Mrs. Eisenhower I saw that her eyes were filling with tears as she talked about General Eisenhower's last years. Anxious to spare her pain, I said "Let's go back to talking about the happy times." "But Barbara," she said, "those *were* happy times. After all, Ike lived to see our son John's book become a success, he lived to see David and Julie married, he lived to see Dick elected, and, most important," she added, laughing out loud with the tears still in her eyes, "he lived to make a hole in one."

Once the hyper-excitement and drama of the funeral is passed, sorrow sets in for a long, heavy stay. There's no way out of it but to endure it.

When you're with someone who has had a recent loss, and wants to talk of nothing else, you're going to have to compose yourself for patient, sympathetic listening. Life isn't easy; every conversation can't be a joy. And in later years, he'll remember gratefully that you listened when he needed you most.

All grief is not for the dead. People show the same symptoms of grief—lassitude, preoccupation with one topic, a general grayness—when they have been through mutilating surgery, or when a marriage or a love affair ends before they were ready, or when they've just moved from a place where they lived long and happily, or when their self-esteem has been punctured by the loss of a job or failure to be chosen for an expected honor.

Be tender; let them tell you how rotten they feel, and what a lousy world this is. Don't argue and try to point out that they have no problems. Sometimes as with teenagers just sympathetically saying, "I know, I know," helps. And have no illusion that they'll be comforted to know you went through something similar—they couldn't be less interested. Also, it's unfair to all concerned to try to share the load by hailing someone over to join you. Psychologists say that one-to-one relationships require the most sensitivity and inner resources of which we are capable—look at the practice you're getting.

Eventually there comes a time when it seems reasonable, at least to you, that the period of mourning should be over. You've heard the same tale of woe twenty times and it's your conclusion that the person is puddling around in delicious morbidity. It's time for him to move on, but you don't want to be ruthless about it.

Remember Mrs. Eisenhower's example, and steer the conversation to talk of the happy times, or comment, "Anyone who has gone through so much must have thought of what can be learned from such an experience. What would you say has been the most useful lesson?"

There's something else that might work. A friend told me this shaggy dog story when I was in my teens and desolated because the current love of my life had just made a date with the high school *femme fatale*. It's about a rich man who hears that there are four words which will explain the secret of life, but they are known only to a very

79

old hermit who is almost impossible to find. The man is so desperate to learn the four magic words that he travels the world over and finally he climbs the highest mountain in Tibet and there, exhausted and penniless, he locates the old man. And the old man haltingly tells him the secret of life, "This too shall pass."

THE HANDICAPPED

A former radio and television actor whose career was ended by Parkinson's disease, the affliction that used to be called "shaking palsy," remarked that handicapped people hate to leave the sanctuary of their homes because of the eyes. There are eyes everywhere, he said: eyes that slide away in revulsion or dislike, eyes that fill with that crippler —pity, eyes that go blank, eyes that stare.

The sweetest encounter he ever had with a stranger occurred in England one evening when he was struggling along a country path. He met a schoolboy of about ten, who watched him with frank curiosity. "Is there something the matter with your leg?" the boy asked conversationally. "Yes," the man replied. "Oh, sir," said the boy, "I *am* sorry."

What the actor found endearing about that simple exchange was its honesty. Handicapped people can learn to cope with their affliction in time, but the embarrassment their affliction causes others is almost unbearable.

The significant factor to keep in mind when talking to someone handicapped is he's *only* handicapped not dying. Don't offer to help unless he asks for it, don't flutter and don't talk in hushed, mournful tones.

Many handicapped people, in fact, are so anxious to put *you* at ease that they are almost too hearty, too outgoing. I'm reminded of Harold Krents, the young blind Harvard student who inspired the 1969 Broadway hit play, *Butterflies Are Free*. I interviewed him on *Today* and he overwhelmed me with ebullience, trying almost too strenuously to stave off any pity I might have been inclined to show.

Then there is the *Today* program's resident gourmet, Roy Andries de Groot, a delightful man and superb cook who happens to be totally blind. I appear on camera with him while he is demonstrating a recipe and we have a matter-of-fact relationship. I asked him long ago his preference about practical matters: would he rather take my arm when leaving the set or have me take his? He'd rather take mine. It makes it easier for him to follow. Since he can't see the hand cues from the crew, I touch his arm to indicate how much time he has left. And before we're on camera, I say to him, "I've put your coffee by your left hand."

It's all simple and minimal. So much so, that most of our viewers have no idea that Roy is blind. He'd rather not be self-conscious about his handicap and all that he requires is that I'm not either.

Perhaps the most difficult interview I ever had on *Today* was with a young man, Robert Smithdas, who was both deaf and blind, a remarkable person who was the only one with this multiple handicap since Helen Keller to get a master's degree. He went further, even, and obtained his doctorate and now helps to teach others who are deaf and blind.

We communicated by his putting his thumb against my lips when I talked. His sensitivity was so acute that he could lip-read that way. Before the interview, his colleagues told me that I should treat him without embarrassment or pity, so I "chatted" with him until he felt at ease with me, and I with him and then I was able to ask him many questions about his personal life and adjustment to his great handicap. I found he wanted me to ask these questions . . . wanted the public to understand.

I concluded by asking what he would most want people to know about his condition and he replied, "Please make it clear that we handicapped are not freaks, but feeling human beings."

In most circumstances where you are uncertain about your behavior, let the other person take the lead. Maybe he'd rather talk of trivialities while you both get your bearings, and maybe he's come to a time and place where he wants to unburden some of his agony. The choice is his, not yours.

We once had Mercedes McCambridge on *Today* and I was introducing her as a fine actress who in the past was an alcoholic. "Not *was* an alcoholic," she corrected me emphatically, "*is* an alcoholic." She began with that to talk about alcoholism and her long struggle with it in a moving monologue that I wouldn't have interrupted if I could. It went on for all the seven minutes of our allotted time, at the conclusion of which I opened my mouth for the first time since the introduction and said, "Thank you, Miss McCambridge." Letters from viewers subsequently confirmed my own feeling that it was one of the most effective "interviews" on *Today*.

In summary, the best advice I can give you is to treat the handicapped person with honesty, which means that you acknowledge that he has a handicap and make whatever adjustments are absolutely essential. But don't make the handicap more important than he is.

It is wise and kind to stay away from the topic of a handicapped daughter or husband, or whomever, when you meet the relatives. If they don't mention the disability in the family of their own accord, consider the subject forbidden. No matter how you think you can legitimize your curiosity by saying you have a friend with a similar situation, you're still taking liberties with private pain.

Increasingly, however, people have a healthy, open attitude about such matters as mental illness or mental retardation in their families. For centuries people had such intense shame about any variation from normal appearance or behavior that the victims were hidden in attics or institutions so relatives could pretend they didn't exist. Joseph and Rose Kennedy, for example, played a significant part in dispelling ancient superstitions and prejudices by refusing to hide the fact of their retarded daughter. Former Vice-President Hubert Humphrey and his wife have also helped in their public acceptance and affection for their retarded granddaughter.

Muriel Humphrey spoke with me of this little girl on *Today* and impressed everyone with her lack of embarrassment or mawkishness. When I asked her about the child, Mrs. Humphrey answered, "Oh, she's just fine. I've been out in Waverly with her and we've had the grandchildren at the lake with us, and Vicky remembered how to swim from last year. And she's growing up to be such a nice young lady. She's seven and a half now and she's learning to read. So she has many possibilities ahead of her. She's doing very well."

I have a special reason for respecting her ready frankness because it is only recently that I've been able to speak of my retarded sister. For a long time, I evaded the subject. If someone asked if I was an only child, I would answer that I had a sister, and if they wanted to know more about her I'd tell them that she lived with my parents, in such a tone of dismissal that the subject invariably was dropped.

I felt I had grown up and accepted the truth of the situation when finally I was able to mention my sister and her condition on the *Today* program, casually referring to her during an interview on mental retardation. I talked of how she herself worked helping to teach young retarded children, and how proud we are of her. My sister, watching at home, was delighted at this recognition, and perhaps we helped others to understand that the retarded have a contribution to make too.

But obviously, to discuss a relative's handicap is a decision that must be made within the individual, consulting whatever wisdom and courage is available. More and more people are making the decision I did, believing that they can ease some of the dark fears by sharing their experience. But many still can't bring themselves to talk about it, and I understand that too.

Never introduce the subject yourself, but if the person you're talking to is able to mention a mentally ill mother or a retarded child, don't flinch. Tell him that you think it is wonderful that he can be so open about it. Encourage him; if more people could stop feeling threatened by such family tragedies, all of society would give a sigh and relax a bit.

But don't canonize him; he doesn't merit the Congressional Medal of Honor for it.

THE BORE

A bore has feelings. Very often he will interrupt something boring he is saying to comment that he is a bore. His wife comes over and inquires sweetly, "Is he boring you?"

If he is, maybe it's your fault. "Being interested makes one interesting," Dr. Erich Fromm observed, to which I would add that you generally get out of a conversation what you put into it.

Regard the bore: he has fashioned for himself a social personality that he hopes will be a winner. He's afraid of awkward silences, afraid of being abandoned, afraid that if he stops talking he will have stopped existing. So he drones on, disgusted with himself but hopeful that this one time people will find him fascinating.

You can bail him out by *insisting* that he be sprightly. The topic he has chosen isn't doing much for either of you, so change it drastically. There are subjects on which he can't be boring because he hasn't talked about them seventy-six times, hasn't even thought about them until you mentioned them. How about, does he think most men are uncomfortable with women? or, why is our society so concerned with hair—is it a sex symbol? or, what teacher helped him the most when he was a child?

You can also try whatever provocative subject is in

85

vogue; there's bound to be one making the rounds, a guaranteed grabber. Some years ago Elizabeth Taylor and Richard Burton were discussed everywhere you went. This was succeeded by the topic of children of prominent people being arrested for taking dope or celebrities having children out of wedlock. Pick whatever is current and choice, and ask the bore to comment on it. What he says may make you angry, but at least you won't be bored.

Is the problem that your particular bore talks so loud that he's giving you a headache? Lower your own voice to a near whisper. It has the effect of making him aware of his noise, in contrast to your softness. Night club singers use the same trick when audiences make too much clatter —they make themselves almost inaudible, and people quiet down to listen.

There are some desperation gambits when all else fails with the bore. If you're eating together, you can try talking about the hospital experiment in which volunteers can select any menu at all, but must eat exactly the same food in exactly the same amounts for thirty days. What would he eat? Ask him if people were colors, what color would he be? What color would his wife be? His boss? If he were an animal, what kind of animal would he be? Remind him that in George Orwell's 1984 the hero and heroine were broken because Big Brother discovered the one thing both dreaded most in the world. What is the one thing he couldn't stand?

Truman Capote has a natural gift that makes him a great guest at a dinner party: he is *always* interested in whomever he's talking to. For one thing, he really looks at the person he is with. Most of us see outlines of one

86

another, but Truman is noting skin texture, voice tone, details of clothing.

My personal experience with his eagle eye occurred a few months after I had interviewed him on *Today* and a year after our negative meeting at Bennett Cerf's house. I arrived at a dinner where Truman was surrounded, as usual, by a group of people enchanted by him. He darted away from them suddenly and came over to me. "Do you remember Tangee Natural lipstick?" he asked. I sure did. "I used to sneak it to school when I was in junior high," I told him, "I would put it on there so my mother wouldn't know. How could I forget Tangee?"

"Well, you should wear it now," he advised me. "I've been trying to remember ever since I last saw you what shade of lipstick would look perfect on you, and I finally got it. It's Tangee Natural, and you must get some." (I searched every five and ten for weeks after, trying to find Tangee Natural without success. I'm terribly flattered that Truman thought so much about me, but couldn't he have suggested Revlon?)

One of the reasons that Truman is always interested in people is that he won't allow himself to be bored. He told me that when he meets a truly crashing bore he asks himself, "Why am I so bored? What is it about this person that is making me yawn?" He ponders, "What should this person do that he hasn't done? What does he lack that might intrigue me?"

He catalogues thoughtfully the bore's face, his hair style, his mannerisms, his speech patterns. He tries to imagine how the bore feels about himself, what kind of a wife he might have, what he likes and dislikes. To get the answers, he starts to ask some of these questions aloud. In

87

short, Truman gets so absorbed in finding out why he is bored that he is no longer bored at all.

THE DRUNK

I'm afraid I don't suffer drunks gladly, even comical ones. There's one variety of drunk who is turning up more and more regularly on the social scene: the woman-hater. He's the kind of man who conceals his resentment of women when he is sober. His wife is washed out, his secretary harassed, and his mother hated him. As he drinks, he gets testier on the topic of pushy women, and when he is ripe he'll find one of the successful women in the crowd and tell her off.

His opening line is, "You're the kind of woman who . . ."

The most graceful rescue I've ever witnessed happened one evening at a party Kitty Carlisle Hart had given. A drunken actor was taking off on me when Kitty suddenly appeared at his elbow. "Oh John," she said to him, beaming, "that's just how you used to insult me. You remember that time at Peter's when . . ." And she led him away, brightly recalling other days and other parties.

If there isn't such a resourceful angel to help you in such a situation, call someone over to join you and the drunk. He will then either stop the personal invective or else the newcomer will come to your support. Try to move the conversation from the particular (you) to the general (life); try to edge the drunk into a larger group. Whatever you do, slip away as quickly as you can and stay out of range for the rest of the evening.

If, on the other hand, the drunk is someone important to you, your boss or a close friend, and you don't want him to be contrite about his condition for the rest of your relationship, *you* pretend to be sick, and leave. The next day you telephone to apologize to him for having to slip away early.

When the drunk is a woman, a particularly unattractive situation, try to help. Tell her the noise of the party is getting you down and you'd like to slip upstairs to a quiet room for a cup of coffee, and would she please come with you? If you were about to leave, ask if you can drop her off and you'll have an opportunity to visit together on the way. Suggest you both find the powder room, and take the long route.

If she won't budge, and as a last resort only, suggest to her escort that he'd better take her home. In the case of a male drunk who is out of control, have his wife or a friend remove him from the premises. In either case, the light touch works best; disdain or anger will make the drunk balk.

I went to a luncheon not long ago where a very famous man got himself drunk with such speed that I was almost impressed. But we all felt embarrassed, and our pretense that nothing out of the ordinary was happening was growing untenable when the celebrity found the solution himself. He turned to another man in the group and said unsteadily, "Will you take me away?" If he hadn't, one of us would soon have invented a pretext for helping him get out with some pride still intact.

THE LECHER

First of all, don't take him seriously. Unless you are alone on the sixth fairway at two in the morning—and how did you get there anyway?—you can always holler. My own opinion is that there's far too little flirtation in our country as is. Most attractive males talk to most attractive women as if they were Rotarians comparing sales percentages in Des Moines. A European, on the other hand, or his rare American counterpart, breathes a little faster when talking to a good-looking woman. His eyes get brighter and somehow, for you anyway, the room gets brighter.

So be grateful. Even a man known to be on the prowl has *some* taste, and he picked you.

If you are the object of a drunken pass, which admittedly is tasteless, don't get angry and tell him off, and don't bring it up the next day. It was annoying, that's true; but don't make a big thing of it.

Most verbal advances are the male's sniff of the wind. Is the girl available, or isn't she? He's entitled to one exploratory maneuver. If you're not available, *really not*, he is likely to feel the total lack of vibrations and drop the pursuit. If you're confused, or if you're feeling lonely at the time, or if you've had a fight with the man in your life and you're thinking of revenge, the Casanova will get the subliminal message that he can proceed. Then if matters get out of hand, it's hardly fair to play the outraged maiden.

Occasionally lechers are so vain that they block out all the negative signals. Then I suggest you try scaring him to death. I knocked off a persistent knee grabber at a dinner party one evening by looking deep into his eyes and purring, "You're absolutely right. We *are* meant for each other. Why don't you divorce your wife and marry me?" A shaken man, he has avoided me evermore.

Into each life, alas, some verbal fists must fall. We all have had the experience, one time or another, of meeting someone whose conversational opener is a kick in the stomach. They start out with something like, "How are the peaceniks making out these days?" or, "You rich people really kill me." A friend of mine who helped to sponsor a youth hostel was asked by a stranger she'd just met, "Are you still hanging around with those long-haired queers?"

The resultant conversation is not likely to be rich in human warmth. Don't waste your charm and logic on him; listen briefly to whatever destruction he stocks and then exit diplomatically by telling him that obviously he has given the matter a good deal of thought and it was interesting to hear his views.

I use the same bland technique, even though my stomach may be churning, when replying to the occasional hate mail I receive on *Today*. After the writer has called me a bore, a hag, a Communist and a Fascist, and sent copies of the letter to all the sponsors, I write, "Thank you for your constructive criticism."

Garry Moore has an even better reply. When the hate mail has been signed (as rarely happens, by the way) he writes the sender, "I think you should know that a madman is writing letters and signing your name."

If, however, you're in a mood for a scrap when someone insults you, and you're sure you can keep your control, go ahead and defend your views. You can't possibly change his mind, but you'll sleep better yourself.

Gossip can be fun when it's gossip about famous people who'll never hear of your discussion and couldn't care less if they did. For me, gossip about Liz and Richard, or Jackie and Ari, is entirely fair, enormously interesting, and probably completely untrue. But gossip about people you know is not only morally wrong, it is also tactically wrong because it almost always gets back to the person involved.

And don't kid yourself into false virtue because you kept silent when others were lacerating someone's reputation. You're never just a spectator: unless you put a stop to it, you're a participant. Change the subject in a firm voice; say, "I like Jane very much and I'm sure none of us here is glad that she's having problems. Let's talk about something else, like what I've been wondering about these past few minutes—who do you think gossips more, men or women?"

I guarantee that the resultant debate will be much snappier than the original gossip.

Of course, there's always the classic line when someone is running down a mutual friend. You look amazed and say, "Funny, she always speaks so well of you." I dare the gossip to go on after that, especially if you follow up your line with a compliment that the friend actually paid the gossip in your hearing.

Conversely, if you meet someone who you've heard has made a bitchy comment about you, try to be big about it. We all have said unkind things that we didn't really mean, tricked by something nervous in the situation or in ourselves. Sometimes people gossip just because they feel they must in order to be interesting.

If the gossip is someone you like and respect normally, tell her or him that you've heard he has a gripe about you and you'd like to straighten it out with him. Maybe it was a misunderstanding which can be cleared up then and there. Or maybe the criticism was deserved, in which case you can learn from it. There *is* such a thing as constructive criticism.

You're only human though, and there are times when it's a strain to be civilized. I had an experience with Joan Rivers before we ever met that made me doubt we could ever be polite, much less pals. She was being interviewed by *The New York Times* on the subject of femininity among female television performers. As examples of tough women, she quipped, "I'd love to put Barbara Walters and Jacqueline Susann in the same room and see which one came out alive."

By a quirk of fate, I had just written Joan what amounted to a fan letter. She was about to do a brand-new interview show on NBC and I wanted to welcome her to the network. She received my note the day before her comment about me was to appear in the *Times* and although we'd never met, she telephoned me in agony to apologize.

I had written the note in all innocence, but I later thought that it was the perfect variation on the "funny-but-she-always-speaks-well-of-you" ploy. Anyway, Joan and I both felt so terrible about the incident that we've been friends ever since.

I once asked Mrs. Spiro Agnew on *Today* about personal criticism, wondering if it bothered her that her husband sometimes received so much of it. She answered serenely and sensibly, "You can't have everyone love you."

Not many people have that much composure. Mrs. John V. Lindsay has a well-deserved reputation for being refreshingly honest. The first time I interviewed her on the *Today* show, I asked what she would do if someone seated her at a dinner party next to William Buckley, who had said cutting things about her husband during their mayorality campaign. Said Mary Lindsay, "I'd get the flu."

PEOPLE WHO REVEAL ALL

From the reporter's point of view, nothing could be finer than a President who replies to a question about his operation by pulling out his shirt and showing the scar. But the news value is absent when an acquaintance at a cocktail party wants to tell you about her alcoholic father or her concern that her husband is impotent.

It may be that the intimate disclosure is of a nature that touches on your experience and you can handle the conversation sympathetically. Then your calm acceptance can be a big help. But keep in mind if you encourage her to talk about the problem that she may hate herself tomorrow morning because she was so frank, and blame you for her indiscretion.

If, on the other hand, you want to beat a retreat from the subject, don't fake understanding. Your discomfort will ultimately show itself and seem like righteousness or rejection. You must divert him at once. Find something positive to say, along the lines of, "I always knew that you were under some kind of strain and I guess almost everyone is, but I admire so much the way you handle your relationship with your children." Or how many activities she juggles without looking frazzled. Or what a helpful person she is, and how people respect her.

If the disclosure is about a marital problem or a falling out between two of your friends, *never referee*. They may forgive one another, but they'll never forgive you. At one point during our engagement, my husband and I decided to break it off. A friend congratulated him warmly, assuring him he was well out of that match. We still see that friend from time to time, distantly.

Tell the wailing one, "I love you both, but I won't let you tell me about this trouble because it hurts me too much." Or say, "I'm not a peacemaker. I'll just stay here on the sidelines and hold both coats."

Shortly after two books about Billy Rose had been published, the two authors appeared on our program. One biography of Billy was by his sister, Polly Gottlieb, and was obviously very favorable; the other was by someone who didn't know him but had written an extremely critical book, calling Billy Rose, among other names, a "robber baron of the arts." Both authors were guests at the same time, and I was trying valiantly to allow each to present his point of view.

Finally, after a particularly biting remark about Billy was made, Polly turned to me and cried, "Barbara, how can you let him say a thing like that! You know Billy just loved you, he treated you like a daughter! Say something." In the *Today* tradition, I rose to great heights of impartiality: "I think," I said, "that it's time for a commercial."

It's curious, but obscene language at social gatherings as often comes from the women as it does from men. I suppose the ladies see it as a mark of emancipation, catching the late comedian Lenny Bruce's technique, but not his message. His use of the four-lettered words was intended to force audiences to confront their stuffiness and prepare them to accept change. The underground press is still mired in the conviction that obscenities is change itself and the hallmark of the revolution.

Adults, however, can surely demonstrate that they are contemporary and liberal with better style. I pay no attention to an obscene word uttered once or twice—it could be a slip, and besides I've read better in books and heard worse in movies. But after the fifth time I say, "If you're trying to shock me, you're not. What you are doing by trying so hard, though, is offending me."

(And often I've been tempted to add, "So screw off.")

Dirty jokes also leave me unimpressed. I've confronted my own stuffiness, and I've decided to keep it.

THE TELEPHONE

Identify yourself at once; the "you'll never guess who this is" opening is a pain in the neck. Give your name clearly and what organization you're with.

Whether you're calling a friend, foe, or stranger, pause after you've stated who you are. It could be a wrong connection or wrong number.

If you have reached the person you want to talk to, you then ask if this is a convenient time for him, or would he prefer that you call back. He could have a crucial decision to make in the next fifteen minutes, or be on the point of leaving for an important appointment. You'll make an impression just by not taking for granted that he was lying there in a hammock, eating chocolates and reading movie magazines, hoping someone would telephone.

Most busy people ask their secretaries to screen their calls, a vital protection against time-wasting, so don't be offended if the secretary wants to know what your call is all about. Tell her, as briefly as possible. If you're after him as a guest speaker at your benefit, or you want a donation or appointment to see him, it's a good idea to write him first with all the details, explaining that you'll be calling him on the phone in a few days for his decision.

After you've identified yourself, paused and made certain that you're not interrupting him, make some appreciative remark about realizing that he's very busy, indicating you'll be as brief as possible.

Finally; be as brief as possible.

how to cope...
with Disaster

Disaster is when you have arrived at a late afternoon wedding wearing your bright red doubleknit, to find all the other guests in long gowns and dinner jackets.

Disaster is when you have picked up a charming ornament and asked the hostess where it came from. She answers, "It was my great-grandmother's," with which you drop it and it smashes to bits.

Disaster is also when you have informed a group of people that you met Mr. and Mrs. Smithright last night, and Mrs. Smithright is a knockout. And a chunky frump says, "That's odd. *I'm* Mrs. Smithright, and I was at home last night."

You can pretend to faint, but this is a temporary measure. You've got to do better than that, and you get marks for quickness. In the first case, I would tell the bride's mother, *once*, that you had to attend another affair and couldn't find time to change without missing the ceremony, which you couldn't bear to do. In the second situation, you apologize to the hostess, who will appreciate how bad you feel, and then prowl the shops the next day until you find something beautiful. Send it to her, with a note that you know it won't make up the loss but you hope she'll enjoy it.

Tell Mrs. Smithright that you must have met another Smithright—is her husband twenty-six, bearded and on crutches from an automobile accident? No? Well, it was someone else entirely then. If it's too late for that, if you've identified him irretrivably, look adorably addled as you remember that the knockout was married to someone else, who soon dragged her off. It probably won't be believed, but it saves Mrs. Smithright's pride.

Some people are socially disaster-prone, like some people have a proclivity for getting into bone-breaking accidents. They're the kind who when talking to a grotesquely fat person find words like "diet" and "overweight" and "blubber" popping into their sentences. Subliminal malice? Maybe.

Shy people suffer another kind of disaster. Set down among people they don't know well, their confidence collapses and they see themselves as the only people in the room lacking wit and grace. Despair sweeps over them, numbing reflexes. They stumble into people sipping hot coffee, and forget the name of their best friend.

Unhappily, most of us have experienced both kinds of disaster. We've all spoken too hastily and tasted our own shoe leather and we've all felt hopelessly inept.

Sometimes the result is so paralyzing that it's impossible to function for the moment. Maybe you'll be lucky and someone with the golden gift of tact will be on the scene. There is a famous illustration of this—the perfect hostess who, when a guest was mortified after knocking over his wineglass, waited a few minutes and then upset hers.

Marian Javits, wife of the senator, saved an embarrassing situation for Johnny Carson at a dinner party we all attended. They were seated beside each other and Johnny, a surprisingly shy and uneasy man in private life, spilled his soup during the first course and later dripped some gravy on his tie. Instead of ignoring it, which wouldn't have improved Johnny's discomfit much, or being solicitous, which would have made him feel worse, Marian made a joke of it all and Johnny joined in until they were both kidding each other.

When something is spilled or broken, the offender is aghast. There's a trace of the child's fear of punishment in his reaction, and a good deal of shame, and anger against himself. It is the obligation of the hostess, *promptly*, to make the person feel as comfortable as possible. Make the broken object seem less important. One heroine cried, "Thank heavens that horror is finally broken. I've hated it for years!" Make the cleanup quick and casual and pick up the conversation where it was interrupted.

If you're the offender and you've broken something that can be replaced, do so as soon as possible. If something has been stained in a spill, perhaps you can have your cleaner pick it up the next day. If these measures aren't feasible, send flowers or a gift, and a note of apology.

Another kind of disaster is the *faux pas*, and I've committed some beauts right in front of the millions who watch *Today*. Not long ago, a guest referred to Albert Schweitzer, and I asked brightly how old Dr. Schweitzer was. The guest looked at me in amazement and said, "But, he'd dead." As I prayed for an immediate power failure, that old wheeze, "I didn't even know he was sick," flashed across my mind, but I knew I had to resign myself to the egg on my face. I confessed frankly, "I'm so embarrassed, how stupid of me. Of course I should have remembered that he died some time ago." And then I asked my next question.

I expected that there would be a landslide of derisive mail, but there wasn't a single letter about my blooper. I think most viewers were sympathetic, maybe having blundered that way themselves once or twice, and perhaps they appreciated my honesty.

The point I want to make is: don't try to bluff your way out unless, as with Mrs. Smithright, someone else's feelings are involved. Admit right away that you made a mistake. You can't lose any more ground than you already have, and you might pick up a little—the ability to say "I was wrong" is exceedingly rare these days and merits respect.

You can cut down the risk of an awkward situation by not asking about an absent spouse unless you know the person rather well. "We're getting a divorce," is a hard act to follow. If it does happen that some remark of yours obliges the other person to explain that his marriage is breaking up, don't say that you're sorry—presumably, he's glad. Say, "Forgive me, I didn't know," and change the subject.

A woman I know was upset for days after making this kind of error. She had just been introduced to a couple, Bill and Nancy, and she couldn't wait to tell Nancy that they had a friend in common, Nancy's former roommate. Nancy looked bewildered for a moment and then explained, "I'm afraid you must be thinking of my husband's *first* wife. She's also named Nancy."

My friend had the aplomb to say, "Well, that's my *faux*

pas for the night," and quickly asked Bill and Nancy where they were living, and if they liked it.

This kind of slip is easily understood, but many come close to being unforgivable. One woman at a dinner party sneered that some task was so simple "even a Mongolian idiot could do it," and later learned that two guests were the parents of a Mongoloid baby. It's best, of course, never to joke about defects. Jerry Lewis's mock-spastic act horrifies me, though I know he is a kind man and a pillar of the muscular dystrophy fund: I wish he wouldn't exploit an affliction to get a laugh.

If you have made such a ghastly blunder, apologize. Tell the people affected that you've learned a lesson, and undoubtedly you have. They'll understand your agony; sometimes very deep friendships begin from such a calamity.

Then there's the time you remark, "I've just read the worst junk you ever saw, Fred Fuller's column"—and a stranger in the group says, "I'm Fred Fuller. Which column do you mean?" When you get your voice back, tell him he's allowed one punch, or tell him you're celebrated statewide for your lack of literary taste, or tell him that you'd be glad to get him a drink because you're on your way to the bar to order arsenic for yourself.

A sweet man I met at a reception told me he watched the *Today* program every morning and had observed the progress of my pregnancy with pleasure as I grew rounder and rounder every passing day until I announced the birth of our baby. Friends of mine who were present became acutely uncomfortable, knowing that our daughter is adopted, but I didn't take offense at all. I realized that the man was only trying to express interest and would feel terrible when he learned his error. I was worried about him.

It's a fact that it is much more comfortable to be in the position of the person who has been offended than to be the unfortunate cause of it. Victims have a moment of hurt and then can display generosity and sweet forgiveness, while the offender is all but destroyed. I notice that people at fault in a situation usually need warmth and support more desperately than the injured one.

If you've made a social blunder, confess and apologize, hoping for graciousness, and then *shut up*. Don't spend the rest of the night describing what you did, trying to wear out the guilt of it by public contrition. Live with your mistake in silence; you'll recover eventually and perhaps be the better for it.

It used to be a major disaster to arrive at a formal party dressed informally, or the other way around, but today almost anything goes anywhere. Hats rarely are obligatory for women, even at funerals and weddings, and only small towns still honor the spanking white kid gloves as the hallmark of a real lady. Most social events draw such a conglomerate of minis, midis, maxis, and pants suits that you can probably wear a nightgown and go unnoticed.

Curiously it now is the men who worry about being dressed appropriately. They dread wearing the only three-piece suit amid the cardigans, or a turtleneck surrounded by ties. At some events, fringed buckskin and gray flannel rub shoulders with mutual unconcern, but in general, most men like the anonymity of dressing like every other man in the room.

I listened to my friend Constance Hope, a top New York public relations consultant and a superb hostess, save the situation for a guest who arrived at her dinner party in a black tie, the only man in formal dress. As Constance greeted him and noticed his embarrassment, she squeezed his arm and murmured, "Good for you. I told everyone that it was black tie but they all forgot. You're the only one who got it right."

If you can't handle how awkward you feel about the way you're dressed, tell the hostess that you have another affair to attend (which will explain your attire) and leave early.

Sickness can be another kind of social disaster. I'll never forget the anniversary party my husband and I gave a few years ago, during a period when New York was having a flu epidemic. All during the day of the party I was kept busy answering the telephone as wives called to say their husbands were sick and couldn't make it or husbands phoned to say their wives had the flu. As the party kept shrinking, I removed place settings and juggled the place cards.

The survivors gathered at the dinner table but in the middle of the soup course, NBC radio's Ben Grauer left the table. I took his temperature, which registered 103. After that other guests began to fold, some of them stretching out on the beds and some on couches. We had invited twenty people, but only eleven finished dinner. I began to feel we were doing a scene from a bad murder mystery.

The role of the hostess in such a crisis is, obviously, to care for her ailing guests. You offer a quiet bedroom, where the guest can lie down for a while. If the sickness is beyond the headache class and he thinks he'd better leave, make certain that transportation is available and that he needs no further help. The next morning you telephone to inquire how he's feeling.

But it is also the responsibility of the ailing guest to cause the minimum of fuss. If you can summon up the stamina, say nothing and stay at the party for a civil length of time. If you're feeling too wretched to last, make your explanation to the hostess inconspicuously and leave without a rollcall farewell of the other guests. Send a note the next day expressing your regret at having to leave such a great party.

If you feel ill before the party starts, call the hostess and tell her "*we* won't be able to come." Don't say "I can't make it," or "George is sick and can't come to your party," because both dangle the suggestion that the healthy person is hoping to go alone. Let the hostess ask you to come by yourself, if that suits her table arrangement or the kind of gathering she has arranged. She is in the best position to decide if a single will fit in, or not.

Another possible upset is the social argument. But I often think that we worry too much about dissension. I lean to the view that a good clash can be wonderfully stimulating, both for the participants and the audience. On the *Today* program we often go out of our way to arrange confrontation. For instance, when the very liberal Dr. Benjamin Spock came to the show to publicize his book *Decent and Indecent*, it was no accident that we also invited the very conservative William Buckley.

When two people are squaring off for an argument, don't feel reflexively that you must stop it at all costs. Size it up. The main consideration, as in the tumbling fights of small boys, is whether someone is likely to be hurt. If the opponents are a good match intellectually, let them go to it.

Don't participate, and don't defend them apologetically; they're big boys.

If you're the one drawn into the argument, make the same evaluation. Can you hold your own? Can the other person? It is only when people feel overmatched, or start to lose, that emotions get out of control.

If the argument deteriorates and becomes personal and vicious, end it at once. "Hey folks," you say in your friendly but strict schoolmarm tone, "this has gone too far. You're making the rest of us uncomfortable, so let's table this discussion for now."

Almost a worse disaster is the group that can't talk at all. There's an anxious silence suffocating the room. People fidget and stare into their drinks. Someone timidly says that the weather has been awful and there's a round of "Hasn't it though," and "You said it," and "Just awful," followed by a long, wretched pause into which someone finally comments, "I was in Tulsa last week and the weather was awful there too." The observation sinks into the silence, and people go back to listening to their ice cubes melt.

The best hope for rescue is an anecdotal question. It will cheer people up to have something happening at last, and give them time to whip up their confidence and enthusiasm. Tell them about a statement you heard on television about some topical matter, and ask if everyone agrees with it. Quote from something you've read about education or automation or violence and ask for an opinion on the subject. Use your family if it can lead to a general discussion—for example, "My teenager came home today and wanted to know if I was a virgin before I was married.

How do you think that should be answered?" I'd love to know myself.

A comedian uses the same sort of trick to get going. He starts with, "A funny thing happened to me on the way to the theater . . ." and from this platform he can launch into any topic he chooses. You can revive a dragging conversation with similar showmanship: the attention-grabbing statement, followed by a question that invites everyone to join in the answer.

It would be a smart move for a hostess, particularly one putting together a group of people who don't know one another well, to make a mental note ahead of time of current news events or some local incident that can be used later to encourage conversation. Don't wait until the emergency occurs—that witty remark about the weather in Tulsa might come from you.

Occasionally you may find yourself talking to someone you just know is lying. Question: Should you tell him that the long anecdotal story he is weaving about himself really happened to your neighbor, and you know it, or should you just sit there fuming inside at his duplicity? In answer, may I turn your attention to Walter Cronkite.

A television critic reporting on the series of television interviews Walter Cronkite did on CBS with former President Lyndon B. Johnson noted admiringly that Cronkite wore "an expression of glazed sincerity as he watched LBJ re-create history."

I say good for Walter Cronkite. I much prefer his technique, rather than directly challenging the person who is being inaccurate or downright fanciful. Unless the lie is derogatory about another person's behavior or involves a matter very important to you, it's a harmless pastime and one most people see through. John Steinbeck never told an anecdote the same way twice and he used to change all the parts around, taking the best one for himself whether he had been present or not. It was entertaining, which was his aim; great story tellers rarely worry about the facts.

Now it's possible that you'll be part of a social disaster some day for which there is no remedy. Not all problems have solutions, and the same is true in human relationships. Resign yourself to the inevitability of a situation for which there is no help at all.

My prime time *faux pas* occurred when I was covering the wedding of Lucy Baines Johnson for Monitor radio. No reporters were allowed inside the church and so, as the invited guests began to exit, I hurried forward to be one of the first to get an on-the-spot account of what had happened. I ran up to a distinguished-looking gentleman with my microphone in hand and said, "I'm a reporter for the National Broadcasting Company. Would you mind telling me please what you think of the wedding?"

"I'm afraid not," he answered. "I'm Frank Stanton, president of the Columbia Broadcasting System."

But that was nothing compared to the experience of a good friend who told me she was talking to an influential man at a party, trying desperately to keep the conversation going, and said idly, "Look at that witch in the polkadots—what a catastrophe she is." And he said, "That's my wife."

My friend asked me what she should have done in the circumstances. I replied, "Kill yourself."

all about You

What you say and how you look are all you have to work with. Fate takes a hand in the matter, giving or withholding such helpful accessories as naturally curly hair, good legs or a small waist, but grooming, personal style, and flair are all up to you.

And, more importantly, so is the personality you project. Psychiatrists, of course, tell us that the fundamentals like anxiety, guiltload, and inner stability are all determined while we're still in diapers, but they also note that every individual designs himself—we are all homemade—and by stubborn will can sort out personality defects and enlarge the best side of himself.

No one goes cradle to grave without ever being unpleasant, cranky, deceitful, and sorry for himself. But the ones we regard as loving and kind are often the ones who give themselves a shake and say, "Stop this nonsense *right now!*" What it takes most is ruthless honesty; you have to be able to see yourself and your behavior as it really is, without the protection of vanity and rationalizing. Let's assume that you're working on the construction of a better version of yourself right now, and that you're making headway.

Even so, the factors that go into the process of two people sizing each other up for the first time are incredibly complicated and subtle. Much of it is chancy: it matters greatly how rested, confident, and healthy each is feeling at the time, since people naturally are less critical of one another when they're feeling in top form.

We can, after all, only judge by an impression that is made then and there. The most off-putting element in anyone you're just meeting is an air of superiority. Often it is the most insecure people who adopt the most imperial manners, because they can't bear to seem vulnerable. But they only succeed in provoking resentment.

On the other hand, the most consistently endearing human trait is warmth. *Everybody* responds to the person who radiates friendliness from a serene core. Such people are lovely to be around because they don't reject or belittle and, best of all, they bring out the best, most generous qualities in the people they encounter, and make them feel marvelous about themselves.

I've been trying to analyze the characteristics of the most charming people I know, hoping to understand what it is about them that makes people go away from them better off than they came. I can name a handful off the top of my head, beginning, first of all, with the men I work with on *Today*. Hugh Downs is unfailingly considerate and polite. It's a fact that we can only tell when he's angry with a guest by noting that he is extra polite and calls him "sir" a lot. Joe Garagiola radiates warmth and makes everyone feel that they've known him for ages.

But I'm not just prejudiced in favor of my cohorts—

there are a number of others I count among the most charming people anywhere—Dorothy Rodgers, Arlene Francis Gabel, Coretta King, the late Bennett Cerf, Kitty Carlisle Hart, Frank Sinatra (when he wants to). They have wildly disparate personalities but what they have in common is the kind of warmth that takes the chill out of the bones of the shyest, most nervous person in the room, and none is snobs.

Let me illustrate, beginning with Mrs. Richard Rodgers because she is, in my opinion, the most charming one of all. Dorothy Rodgers is the wife of the composer and a singularly graceful author herself. One time a few years ago, when we didn't know the Rodgerses very well, my husband and I were invited to their famous Christmas Eve party, at which the Rodgerses enfold family and friends and strays.

My husband's teenage daughter, Carol, was visiting us for her school vacation and we left her reluctantly to go to the party. When Dorothy greeted us and asked about our family, I told her that Carol was with us for a few days.

"She must come to our party," Dorothy said, and insisted that we telephone her to join us. I thought it was a remarkably kind gesture, but Dorothy Rodgers went further. When Carol arrived Dorothy left her other guests who included Danny Kaye, Mary Martin, Betty Furness and some forty others, and spent a relaxed five minutes with Carol, asking her about her school, what she was studying, what she thought about what she was doing. She took the time, and seemed unhurried about it, to make Carol feel comfortable. I can't count how many times I've seen Dorothy Rodgers show that kind of consideration for people, but I'll never forget the incident with Carol.

Arlene Francis is another with the magic ingredient of warmth. Unlike so many performers, she's exactly the same off the camera as on. She has great wit, often at her own expense, and my husband also claims that she's one of the sexiest women he knows. She too gives time generously when she meets people—she doesn't fly around, waving, grinning and distractable, but sits concentrating on her conversation with you until it is finished.

Kitty Carlisle Hart is adored by everyone. A widow for almost a decade since her brilliant husband Moss Hart died, she has never suffered the fate of so many widows, who are dropped socially. She goes to almost every glittering party given in New York and most of the select intimate ones, because she can always be counted on for good spirits and zest. She's the kind of person who always laughs at your jokes. And when she goes out lecturing, people are bowled over by her genuine interest in their community, especially the schools and other facilities for children.

When Kitty was having a minor problem with a teenage son, minor and temporary, she shared it with people and made them feel that their own difficulties were maybe only routine. I think I can sum her up best by saying that after you've talked a while with Kitty, you like yourself more.

I want to emphasize that none of these ladies is a silly, gushing phoney. They are all poised, sincere, intelligent, and they all reach out to others not only because they are built that way, but because they make an extra effort.

Bennett Cerf's most noticeable characteristic was his curiosity. A celebrity himself, he was nevertheless frankly thrilled to meet other celebrities. But celebrity or not, he was endlessly fascinated by people, all kinds of people—rich, poor, old, young—and he wanted to know how they lived, what they ate, how they felt about themselves sexually, what was happening in their families. My husband and I gave a large party one time and my secretary, Mary Hornickel, came to help me with the guests. The next day I asked her if she had enjoyed herself and whom she'd met. I wasn't surprised when she said she'd had a long talk with Bennett—he had wanted to know how she got her job, what she did, how she liked it, what boy friends she had. She was absolutely charmed with the frank attention and interest.

Bennett's questions were always like that, penetrating and sometimes outrageously personal, but people realized that he was truly interested and paid attention to what they said and they basked in his presence. He could communicate with anyone, from his most important authors to strangers who stopped him on the street for his autograph. He was in his seventies when he died, but he was the youngest man I knew.

Phyllis Cerf, Bennett's wife, is also an unusually outgoing woman. She too is interested in all kinds of people but seems to have a special talent with young people . . . even very young people. She captivated my little girl one evening by kneeling on the floor and patiently explaining what every item in her evening purse was. My Jacqueline was so pleased with the nice lady's concentrated attention that she didn't even try to eat Phyllis's lipstick. But if you really want a personal reference on Phyllis Cerf, you should ask no better an authority than Frank Sinatra. He's mad about her.

Which brings me to my own experience with Sinatra. It is true that Frank Sinatra rudeness is legendary. But his old-fashioned courtliness is rarely written about. I can vouch for the fact that he treats most women as if they were made of glass, as concerned for their comfort and dignity as a

Victorian. He has another little-known quality—grace. My husband and I were strangers to Frank when we attended the same party some years ago. We were standing some distance apart, very much aware of his famous face, when he disarmed us by approaching with a warm smile, putting out his hand and saying, "I'm Frank Sinatra. How do you do."

I also value him for his compassion. I told him once that my retarded sister was a great fan of his. He then took the trouble to write her a personal letter crammed between the lines with kindness.

Just recently he charmed me again by watching *Today* every morning during a period when he was in Arizona and sending, via Bennett Cerf, some constructive criticism that I very much appreciated. He said I was too deadpan when I talk, which is true. I'm working on it, pleased and flattered that Frank Sinatra has concerned himself about me.

Coretta King, widow of Martin Luther King, Jr., is another who projects love. She recently wrote to me about a project of mutual interest and included in the letter a description of the doings of her four children. Knowing of my particular affection for her youngest daughter, Bunny, Mrs. King wrote: "Bunny has not yet changed her ambition to be a policewoman. She is having a grand time this summer and growing unbelievably fast."

The personal comments about each child made me feel even closer to Mrs. King, who ended her letter, "Give my best regards to your own family and to your secretary, Mary."

Martin Luther King, Jr., talked about the power of love to change the world, but his wife uses it on a one-to-one basis that is wholly healing. She's full of toughness and courage, as she has demonstrated, but her nature is tender and sweet—and there is nothing on earth more charming than a loving woman.

My friends are incredulous that I add President Richard Nixon to this list. Even his admirers tell me they find him cold and stiff and his detractors, of course, use more interesting language. I can't verify the accuracy of any such descriptions because I only know that you take people the way you find them, and I was charmed by him when we first met.

The first occasion was in the White House when I was interviewing his daughter Tricia for *Today*. President Nixon came out of his office unexpectedly and joined us, and I asked him if I could have my picture taken with him. It was a corny request maybe but the President couldn't have been more courteous. He took me into his office and put me at my ease by telling me that I was sitting in the same chair occupied the week before by Mrs. Golda Meir, the Prime Minister of Israel. With this opening, we talked for several minutes about her and her country's problems and I was grateful that Mr. Nixon was making it so easy for me to be with him.

This, by the way, was the conversation that led to the President obtaining Prince Philip's acceptance of my invitation to interview him on *Today*.

The next time I saw Richard Nixon was just before a White House dinner for Andrew Wyeth, when the President lingered much longer than his aides wanted him to with a group of women reporters. Many people have been surprised when I talk about his informality and friendliness then, claiming that he was just buttering up the press, but I've known a great many important people who have never bothered to be gracious on such occasions.

I haven't talked with Richard Nixon in years and I doubt that he would be as tolerant of the press today, but I remember the past and it was nicer then.

Summing up my favorite charming people, I realize that each of them invests *time* in even casual relationships. They're all busy, with heavy demands on them, but they all have the knack of making it seem that clocks and pressures don't exist because it is so wonderful to be talking to you, no matter who you are. Educational psychologists, referring to the attitudes of teachers toward students they like and students they dislike, use the terms warm time and cool time; charming people live mostly in warm time.

About the least charming people I know are actors and comedians. Marlon Brando has been quoted as saying, "Movie stars aren't mature as people. No actor is. Ever meet an actor who's really worth talking to offscreen or offstage? Ever meet an actor who was a whole person without his image up there for you to fill in?"

It's generally true. Actors, with few exceptions, are self-centered, morose and easily affronted when they slip out of their professional personalities and try to carry on a conversation on a one-to-one basis. They aren't interested in anyone else but themselves and they take no trouble to conceal their boredom when the topic wanders from their favorite subject.

I exclude from this generalization almost all the new young anti-actors, who live very involved lives away from the cameras and haven't altogether lost their perspective. It came home to me when I watched Dyan Cannon and Jon Voight accept their New York Film Critics awards.

118

Neither of them bothered with that fatuous and transparently insincere parade of producers, directors and assorted husbands who made it all possible. Instead they spoke simply about how they felt, and everyone who heard them felt their joy too.

Undoubtedly inner confidence is the key to making genuine contact with another person. Nervous people are too involved with their own alarm bells and flashing signals. In any new encounter, you have valid reason to be concerned, if only because your self-esteem sags so badly when you know you haven't made a good impression. If an additional strain such as meeting your husband's boss or your boy friend's mother is added, you can be in real trouble.

To offset some of the panic, assess the situation ahead of time. What is the worst thing that can happen? Try to envision what it is and consider how it can be handled. Perhaps you dread being thought of as stupid and uninformed; if that's the case, plan ahead of time what subjects you can discuss comfortably and try to bring them up—and vow that if the topic gets out of your field you'll be candid and say, "I'm interested in what you're talking about, but I'm ashamed to say that I don't know much about it." Don't bluff: there is no surer road to ruin.

If the worst that you can imagine is the fear of arriving at a party where you don't recognize a soul and you're left orphaned by the door, analyze that possibility. It won't last long, though it may seem forever, and you can stall away a few minutes by being busy selecting hors d'oeuvres or checking in your purse for a handkerchief. Find a telephone and make a call, hoping the situation will have improved when you're finished. You can also take a deep breath and join the least formidable cluster of guests, introducing yourself with as agreeable and relaxed an expression as you can muster. Most people know how tough it is to break into a party and will be kind.

Nervousness causes some people to become helplessly garrulous. They listen in horror to their own voices going on and on, trying to rescue one silly wrong-taste remark with another that turns out to be worse. If this happens to you, try to steady yourself by taking deep slow breaths. Deep breaths are very helpful at shallow parties. It also helps to be just plain candid. I liked the heroine in a recent novel who said, "Forgive me for talking so much. I always do that when I don't have anything to say."

Some people have an opposite reaction when nervous. They retreat into themselves, pulling down all the shades. The meek mouse approach won't give offense to anyone, but it lessens the likelihood that you'll enjoy yourself. Get your courage up and participate: it's like exercising a muscle, the more you do it, the better it works.

A television performer friend of mine gets her composure together before a show by saying over and over, "*They can't kill me.*" My own talisman is Abigail McCarthy's serene observation, "I am the way I am; I look the way I look; I am my age."

If nothing works, admit frankly that you're nervous. It is a refreshing admission that brings out the protective instinct in others, because everyone knows how miserable it is to be tense and fearful. *Everyone.* James Stewart was a guest on the *Today* show when he brought the revival of *Harvey* to the Broadway stage, and he confessed he was almost paralyzed with stage fright on his opening night. If he can admit it, so can you.

There's another situation that puts a strain on your resources and that is going on when you feel just rotten. I think we've all wondered how, for example, women acrobats or high board divers manage to perform when they're having their periods, and we've all endured less dramatic experiences ourselves with the same problem. You wake up feeling awful, with a cold, or cramps, or remorse, but you're required to turn up at work or a party looking vivacious and carefree. How do you do it?

You just do, that's all. Sometimes when I wake up at 4:30 A.M., I feel I can't possibly wash my face, brush my teeth, put on clothes and make-up and smile for everybody at 7:00 A.M. But I must, so I do. I try to take one thing at a time, telling myself that if it's absolutely, positively necessary, I'll go home right after the show is over. But by 9:00 A.M., I've usually forgotten all about my pre-dawn aches and pains. So don't worry about how you're going to feel at 7:00 P.M. when it's only 7:00 A.M. If your day is too crowded, cancel the one unnecessary appointment that's. making it all too much. But don't mope around the house when you're low or you'll wind up feeling worse. Get to your feet and get moving: it's the best tonic available.

Wear your most smashing outfit: maybe something a bit kooky that you'll have to live up to. If you're concerned about perspiration or other stains, choose something that will give maximum concealment. A woman I know who does a lot of public speaking always has one terrific red dress in her wardrobe to wear on the dangerous day of her period.

When you finally get out of the house, don't talk endlessly about how lousy you feel. It's a waste of time and will only make you feel less capable of going on.

Arlene Francis wrote a useful book about charm a few

121

years ago which included her own prescription for over-coming the blahs. She pretends she's in a good mood, disciplining herself to smile and be outgoing. Eventually, because her smile is contagious, everyone in the room starts beaming too and she discovers that somewhere in the interval, her own smile became genuine.

Occasionally it helps to have something to eat. Food clearly has a therapeutic value in times of stress—depressed people can console themselves into obesity and funerals are followed by feasts. Try food in moderation. A good break-fast will offset the midafternoon droops, for instance, and the classic cure-all of hot chicken soup is not just a joke. It really is a kind of mothering. Even if you're dieting, give yourself one day off; call it Mental Health Day.

I hate to suggest that a drink or even six is the answer. I don't notice that people cope better after a few "medic-inal" nips and, more often, the reverse is true. But if you think that one drink will perk you up, go ahead; but stop at one.

Don't ever underestimate the importance of being rested. (This is one time I don't practice what I preach, but I wish I could.) From personal experience, I know that great fatigue brings on depression. You feel as if you're ill and if somebody touches you, you'll cry. But even when you're just vaguely tired, it is more difficult to be patient, under-standing, or enthusiastic.

Get some of the trivia out of your life and substitute rest. Make a list sometime of all the situations that loosen tension for you. With some people music works, others watch clouds, or look through antique shops, or walk on beaches. My release is to take my little girl to the park. It's an entirely different world there. Whatever your release is, put it on the agenda regularly and give it the highest priority in your life. It's the smartest investment you'll ever make.

There's a gimmick I use for emergencies when I need to recover my sense of well-being in a hurry. I follow the suggestion that photographers give their subjects when they're posing in front of the cameras and looking glum. They're told, "Think of the happiest moment you've ever had," or, "Think of the person you love most in the world." When you do this the tension goes out of your posture and your face, and softness floods in. You look and feel refreshed.

It's really a form of method acting. You re-create the best version of yourself by remembering when you felt your best. When in trouble, try to re-enact the luminous, loving you.

Your appearance plays an important part in the impression other people have of you, but maybe not the way you think it does. Women often concentrate on details like matching accessories or adjusting hem-length, while missing the point. The way you dress is the billboard that tells perceptive people how you feel about yourself. Very feminine women float around in a drift of apricot chiffon and stylish, no-nonsense women have beige and black wardrobes with interchangeable parts. Impulsive ladies have the wildest collections, ranging from dresses fit for a nunnery to spangles and fringe.

I'm all for the wardrobe that expresses a point of view; too many women blank themselves by dressing like the herd. These are usually the same ladies who may have opinions on controversial matters but keep them demurely to themselves. It's *so* ladylike—and boring.

Try to get a concept of yourself when you buy clothes.

Don't overlook your silhouette: hem-length determines the kind of shoes you wear, for instance, and you can only have bulk one place at a time—a chunky coat means a small hat.

Don't spend your energy on trying to compensate for a figure or facial defect. If it's something that can't be changed, accept it. You're an individual and not someone stamped out of a mold at a doll factory. Besides, imperfections can add up to stunning beauty—look at Sophia Loren's face, with the too-generous mouth and slanted eyes. For heaven's sake, look at Barbra Streisand. If their faces were perfect, they would look ordinary.

When you're apprehensive about something you're about to do, dress on the conservative side. You may not stand out but you'll feel more confident. Pastels are pretty and feminine (I've noticed over the years that First Ladies very often choose yellow for their Inaugural Ball gowns) and black or white is always good. Wear at least a small sleeve—sleeveless dresses can be harsh. And keep the clutter to a minimum.

A nervous-making situation is no time for a new dress, even though that's what we usually think will help. Dorothy Rodgers always wore the same thing, a simple gray jersey, when she attended her husband's opening nights. She says there was enough of a strain on those evenings without the complication of trying to break in a new dress.

Henry David Thoreau had similar doubts: He wrote gloomily in *Walden*, "Beware of all occasions requiring new clothes."

In my opinion, the most important investment you can make in your appearance is a hair-do. If you have a spare hour before some event and you think you might spend it shopping for a scarf or shoes to improve your outfit, don't. Go to a hairdresser instead. Hair is the sexiest ornament you have.

I sometimes jokingly maintain that saran wrap and electric curlers are the world's two greatest inventions. The curlers are indispensable to me professionally, and I never travel without them. Because of electric curlers, I rarely have to go to a professional beauty salon or sit under a hot drier. I wash my own hair and towel it dry every two or three nights before I go to bed. The next morning, it is rolled up on electric curlers for about ten minutes, combed out, and I'm ready to go on the air. I also recommend the purchase of a good fall or wig. There are so many variations of these hair pieces, from clip on pony tails to a full head of hair that slips over your own like a bathing cap. And now with synthetic hair, the prices couldn't be more reasonable. Especially in cold weather I like the kind of hat you can tuck all your hair into as an emergency measure. Big furry hats are great hair tucker-inners in the winter.

You'll have to figure out your own version of what-to-do-until-the-hairdresser-comes, but make sure that you have a bag of tricks for emergencies. *Nothing* makes you prettier than fresh, shining hair; dull, dowdy hair will cancel out a size-five figure, a thousand dollars of Paris pink silk and three hilarious jokes about Spiro Agnew. Get your hair done, or buy a good, easy-to-care-for wig.

I think I could write an entire book about make-up. Like all performers I am required to know what new techniques and materials are available. I also pay particular attention to how other women apply their make-up, looking for ideas,

125

and I've come to the conclusion that we're all reading too many books and magazine articles on the subject. The result is that we end up looking like an exaggerated Richard Avedon portrait in *Harper's Bazaar*. And that's great for selling magazines but not so great for walking down the street.

One example that particularly bothers me: these days too many women go out with great blobs of white under their eyes. We've all read that white under the eyes reduces the shadows. But this kind of shading takes a light touch and an expert's hand. If you want to use this or any other kind of make-up shading trick, learn to trust what your own eyes tell you. Take your mirror to the window. No cheating. Pull the shade up. If you can see white under your eyes, so can everyone else. The same goes for too much rouge or eye shadow. At night, you can use a heavier hand for a more dramatic effect, but not in the daytime.

I would steer away from false eyelashes for the same reason; they're false and they look it. Judith Crist, Aline Saarinen, and I all used to wear them on *Today*, but now we neither wear them on camera or off.

In general, beware of too many tricks unless your time is unlimited. Gloria Vanderbilt Cooper always looks devastating. Her make-up is superb. But she has admitted in magazines to spending over an hour just putting on her face.

The rest of us can do best with a good base and then one of the soft blush powders or gels, because they look so natural, and some eyeliner. I use roll-on mascara and then powder over it, to avoid the spikey look, and then more mascara. I don't like colored eyeshadow myself but stick to light brown or gray, on camera and off in the daytime, and a whiter eyeshadow at night—not dead white but white with a colored undertone. The light shade for night has the effect of making your eyes look brighter.

Only young girls can get away with the pale no-color gel lipsticks. As we get older, we need more color. I wear a peachy-brownish shade on television, and off I wear a somewhat brighter shade. I always wear eye make-up with it. I consider it as important as lipstick. I don't bother with a lipstick brush or those fussy tricks with two shades of lipstick; to me that's a waste of time.

Perfume is lovely, but most women have been oversold by the advertisements and wear too much. (I never believed that her perfume had anything to do with the violinist sweeping that girl off her piano bench.) And besides, it can be very expensive. A perfumed bath oil can be dabbed on just like the actual perfume and its scent will last almost as long. But it costs a whole lot less. I also like spray-on colognes or I buy an inexpensive atomizer top and put it on the regular cologne bottle so I can spray it on all over. With scented bath oil and matching cologne, you really don't need to spend the extra dollars on expensive perfume. If you go to work in the morning, leave off the perfume. I think most men find strong perfume somewhat nauseating first thing in the morning. I start to dab it on me about two hours after I arrive at work on *Today*.

I assume you're bathed, deodorized and sweet breathed, so you're all set for hours of superb conversation. The way you look, shining pretty and friendly, people are going to gravitate toward you even before you open your mouth. And when you say to the statesman, "Do you believe in immortality?"—you'll have it made.

8
how to win...
A New Boss, or Husband

There are a few times in your life when it isn't melodramatic to say that your destiny hangs on the impression you make. Such times include the mating season and job-hunting, but there are also a scattering of other fateful encounters, such as when you need a big backer for a cultural project or an opinion-maker's support for a campaign.

At moments like these, you're not interested in second place. It's good enough for cocktail parties and ladies' luncheons to be just agreeable, but crucial situations require more of everything—especially poise.

It is almost impossible to maintain poise when you are scared to death. My best advice for dealing with destructive anxiety is *homework*. Like an orator with a well-worn speech, an actor who is thoroughly rehearsed or a schoolboy with history dates neatly printed on his palm, preparedness is the best technique for reducing panic and enabling the real, lovable you to function.

Homework helps enormously when you apply for a job. First, it's a good idea to prepare ahead of time a resume of who you are, what your education has been, and what you've done professionally so far. Then take pains to find out something about the company you're approaching. In a small community, someone in the same field can supply the information. Local reference libraries can provide the broad background from their files of business and professional journals. If possible, talk to someone who already works there. Does the company prefer employees who are crisp and detached, or employees who fit into the one big happy game? What is the tempo of the company? Does the personnel director have any ardent likes or dislikes?

Homework also can be used to impress a distinguished person you know you are going to be meeting. Do some advance research about him, looking for the off-beat and less celebrated interests he may have. And although I admit that it's kind of sneaky, homework can help you make an impression on the new man you've just met or are trying to meet. If you want to claim his undivided attention, and you do, try to find out in advance what his hobbies and enthusiasms are. Bone up on them yourself and you'll be way ahead of the game, at least at the beginning.

I've developed some general rules as a result of my experience as an interviewer on the *Today* show these past six years, and they can be as useful to you when you're faced with a job interview or a prospective love affair as they are to me when I want someone as reticent as, say, Fred Astaire, to open up. I summarize them in the words of the traffic warning we learned as children: Stop, Look, and Listen.

I've dealt already with Stop: It means, *do your homework*; know as much about the situation as you possibly can. It also means that you don't hurl yourself into some profound or startling topic right away. On *Today*, I talk to the guest I'll be interviewing for a few minutes before we go on camera, to give us both a chance to adjust to one another's style and pace. And unless time is very limited, I try not to launch the televised part of the interview with a weighty question; it's too soon and will jolt the guest and make him defensive.

A warm-up period of small talk between strangers gives each time to make those mysterious little adaptations that result in what we then call being on the same wave length.

There is a psychologist at York University in Toronto, Dr. Vello Sermat, who spent four years developing a test to help explain how people become friends. He's applying it now in his research center and estimates that he'll have the answer in about ten or fifteen years. While we wait, I only know that strangers have to get used to one another for a few minutes before anything can begin, and small talk is more socially acceptable than feeling and sniffing.

The next point is to Look. Give the person you're with the flattery of your total attention. Don't let your eyes stray to see who has just come in or what's happening across the room. The most charming people I know give the impression that they've waited all day to speak to me alone. For the moments that we're talking, no one and nothing else is important. Even in a crowded room, we seem to have isolated ourselves.

My father Lou Walters, a well-known show-business producer, has complained many times that he sees only my profile when I'm doing a television interview. "You should cheat," he grumbles paternally, meaning that I should turn my head away from my guest and look at the camera when asking my questions. I've explained to my father that it's essential to the rapport I must establish

131

that I look right into the face of the person I'm interviewing. As a matter of fact, before we start we say to the usually apprehensive guest, "Don't pay any attention to the lights and cameras and stage manager—just look at us and let the camera eavesdrop on our conversation."

By keeping my eyes on the guest, he keeps his eyes on me and forgets he's in a television studio. He relaxes and talks at ease and, after the interview is over, most of our guests say "That wasn't so bad!" or, "It went so quickly!"

The same guidelines work in a social situation. Unless the house catches fire, keep your eyes firmly on the face of whomever you're talking to.

The last point is to Listen. Not to pretend to be listening, but to really listen. We've all heard the kind of interviewers who are so nervous or preoccupied with their list of prepared questions that they don't hear what the subject is saying. It goes like this: "I see you've been married for six years. How is your wife?" "I killed her last week, as a matter of fact." "Glad to hear it! And how are the children?"

I know a girl who swears that she went through an entire cocktail party replying gaily "I'm dying," whenever anyone asked "How are you?" All evening long, people responded vaguely with, "That's good," or "You certainly look great." She was amused at first, but later awfully depressed at the whole business.

It is also important to judge what kind of person you're with, as well as what he is actually saying. Trust your instincts: Is he open or shy? Can you get personal or should you stick to neutral subjects?

I had a fine interview with Fred Astaire because what

132

he was not saying seemed more important to me than what he *was* saying.

Knowing that he is a very private man, I had researched the events of his life and prepared a long list of questions so that I would have sufficient material even if he answered each tersely.

The interview began as I suspected it would, with quiet, shy, polite answers from Mr. Astaire that revealed nothing about the man himself. This was not, I decided, going to be a winner, so on impulse I threw away my planned questions and announced that he seemed to me totally lacking in the usual actor's ego. For example, he rarely used the word "I."

Right away the atmosphere changed. I listened with new interest as the usually introverted Fred Astaire admitted, "I've never thought about that before but it is true. I am uncomfortable with people who are analytical and self concerned." He later went on to reveal that he had a clause in his will which forbade anyone ever making a movie out of his life story. He explained that he'd watched Irene Castle's unhappiness over the motion picture of her life with Vernon which she felt distorted them. He decided then to protect himself from the usual Hollywood treatment of a life story. "My life is too simple," he said. "I was only married once. I loved my wife. She died. How would Hollywood blow that up?"

Because I had used my intuition about his character, Fred Astaire came off as aware and sensitive as he really is beneath the shy exterior.

But there are times when, no matter how intuitive or sensitive you are, you have trouble drawing a person out. He is shy or inarticulate and needs a little encouragement.

NBC's Frank McGee told me of a trick he practices when interviewing someone who is hesitant or unsure. When there is a pause, Frank will say, "Really, I never knew that." It makes the person feel as if he has just said something extremely interesting and he may well have. He then goes on to continue his observation with more confidence and animation, feeling happy with himself and Frank.

From my own experience, I would say that few television interviewers are more encouraging to talk with than David Frost. Not only does he never take his eyes from your face, but by his smiles, nods, and warmth of expression he makes you feel as if everything you say is worthwhile and entertaining. It is no wonder that so many guests on his program find themselves saying, "I've never told anyone this before."

Compliments are also helpful when you want to endear yourself to someone, but there's a trick to the whole business. Try not to compliment in a generalization, such as "You're just the best writer in the world!" or, "You're such a *marvelous* person!" It's unimaginative, in the first place, and jangles with insincerity.

The intent of the compliment is to make the person feel that you admire him for who and what he is, so it doesn't serve its function unless it demonstrates that you know something specific about the person, something that sets him apart.

Again, my friend, child psychologist Haim Ginott maintains that the wrong kind of praise can do more harm than good. Working with children he found that vague overblown compliments made them feel guilty and undeserving. His advice . . . compliment the action or the deed not the child. Example: if your child has just removed all of the dead leaves from the back yard, don't say, "You're without a doubt the best child in the whole world," say, "You did a wonderful job of cleaning up the yard. It never looked better."

He applied the same theory to criticism, which few people handle well. "Criticize the deed," says Dr. Ginott, "not the doer."

There is also the third person method of criticism, I mentioned earlier. You have met a flaming radical, let's say, and you find to your surprise that you like him and you want him to like you, but his political stance bothers you. You don't say, "You people are tearing down society with no idea of what you'll put in its place"; you say instead, "Some people think" or "There are those observers who say that the trouble with the radical movement is that it has no solutions." You've dealt with the issue you dislike, but you've left the man himself intact to defend it.

On this subject, don't make the mistake so common these days of judging on the basis of appearances; you could be dead wrong, and it isn't going to be easy to remain convincing if you have to change social gears.

Hugh Downs once commented that people take him for the perfect representative WASP, White Anglo-Saxon Protestant. "But none of this is really true," he protests. "I am not white because no one truly is. I have two parents, four grandparents, eight great-grandparents and so on back. If I were to trace my lineage through generations, it is not likely that I would be totally white.

"I am not Anglo-Saxon. I am Celtic.

"I am not a Protestant because I am not an adherent

of the Christian faith in a formal way. I am more inclined to the Buddhist outlook.

"Yet most people would describe me as a WASP."

There's another hazard to guard against when the conversation is vital to your future—the use of pretentious language. A great many people think that polysyllables are a sign of intelligence and refinement so they think they will impress others with their command of obscure words.

Our U. S. Ambassador to Britain, Walter H. Annenberg, unfortunately gave an all-too-clear illustration of contrived language when he was presented to Queen Elizabeth and she asked a simple question about his housing arrangements. He replied, "We are in the ambassadorial residence, subject of course to some of the discomfiture as a result of the need for elements of refurbishing and rehabilitation." He meant, "We're redecorating right now, so the house is in a bit of a mess."

Stick to good, solid words that say what you mean as directly as possible. It's the language of poets and all people who want to be understood.

WHEN TO BE SEXY, AND WHEN NOT

When not is when applying for a job, or when trying to keep one. Employment offices agree that the beddable look does not lead to the door marked *President* but to the one marked *Exit*. Be sexy on your own time; working hours and job interviews require the crisp and cool version of you.

The main element in landing the job is, believe it or

136

not, how badly you want it. Employers these days put a premium on enthusiasm and zeal because they are fed up with employees who regard their jobs as places to display their wardrobes while waiting for life to begin at five o'clock.

Your initial interview is concerned with your qualifications, and it's a poor idea to fake experience you haven't had, but your attitude matters more. Are you really interested in working for this company? Are you interested in working at all? Have you ambitions about being promoted and, if so, to what?

Have the job specifics straight. Is it within your qualifications or are you hoping to bluff for as long as it takes you to learn on the job? If the job interview has you terrified, maybe it's because you know at the bottom of your mildly larcenous heart that you really aren't ready for the position. Back off and try for a job you're sure you can muster with only a little stretch.

But if this one is for you, don't overdo ambition. Personnel directors calculate that whatever impression you make during the employment interview will be magnified when you land the job. An aggressive edge therefore will lead them to suspect that you'll be a real dragon if you get the job.

You're not making a social call when you apply for a job, so don't be cozy. Comments about the office furnishings or what the interviewer is wearing are inappropriate. In the same vein, don't be too confiding. The question, "Are you married?" requires only a yes or no, not a recital of your divorce action.

Play it safe when you dress. Wear stockings; don't wear a pants suit; go easy on the make-up and perfume and

137

hair-do. Be clean—if you can't decide whether or not a dress looks fresh enough to wear one more time, it doesn't.

There are some questions *you* should ask. For your own decision making, you should know about salary range in your job category, what benefits are available, what services and activities the company offers, the turnover rate and the opportunities for advancement. It will establish that you're serious about yourself and what you do, a big plus. But don't spend all your time asking about insurance benefits, vacations and promotions.

You have to pack a lot of information about your good qualities into a brief time, so the most efficient way to demonstrate that you're reliable and self-disciplined is to be on time. It's a good idea to arrive about five minutes early, in fact. If you're kept waiting past your appointment and it's going to make you late for something else, don't hesitate to explain that you're expected somewhere else and must leave in time to make it. It's the Swiss train trick —people adore the trains in Switzerland because they are *on time*. If you can rearrange your later appointment, ask to use the telephone and do so. Dependable, that's you.

Some job interviewers are deliberately cold to determine whether your composure will stand up to it. Don't get angry and don't get anxious; wait it out. And if the job interviewer takes the pals-together approach, don't be misled into telling her or him *all*. One girl lost a job she wanted badly because she felt cozy enough with her perspective boss to tell him that her hobby was witchcraft. In particular withhold the turgid details of your family or emotional hangups; that's the kind of information that will label you a bad risk.

And don't spoil your whole day expecting the worst

because the interviewer was brief. Long interviews don't necessarily mean you have it made. Years ago I went with a friend to be interviewed for admission to Sarah Lawrence College. My friend was in the admissions office for an hour and when my turn came I was there only ten minutes. I *knew* I'd be turned down. But I was accepted and she wasn't.

If you're applying for a job from a woman, examine yourself candidly to decide if you have some prejudices about a lady boss or not. Having worked for some wonderful women like Eloise McElhone and Anita Colby I feel myself that a woman often makes a better boss than a man: she is more likely to be considerate about such matters as getting your hair done or having the baby sitter fail to show up. She is also more likely to be a well-organized person and realistic about what to expect from others. In addition, I'm told by my own secretary that women dictate more slowly than men. Don't dismiss the idea of working for a woman too quickly.

Besides, the woman boss eliminates the usual office game of light or heavy flirtation. With apologies to Helen Gurley Brown, I think that an office affair is the kiss of death, as far as your job is concerned, that is. Most bosses are married men and so, unless it turns out to be for keeps and he goes the whole route of divorcing his wife and marrying you, the only way to end the affair will be to fire you.

This doesn't mean that you shouldn't be feminine. I am the only woman among the *Today* show's regulars and I was hired because I am a female. I'm often asked if working with men presents any difficulties and I answer truthfully that Hugh Downs, Joe Garagiola, Frank Blair, and I get along marvelously, and that the two hours we spend together on air each morning is the easiest and pleasantest part of my working day.

Why? Well, first of all, we're courteous and considerate. When we see one another at five-thirty every weekday morning we always say good morning and how are you. We all speak softly and if one or the other of us doesn't want to talk, we respect that.

Next, we're honest with each other. We speak our minds if we think we should be included in an interview or if we want to do it alone. In the more than six years that Hugh and I have worked together, we've never had an argument, but this is because of our mutual respect rather than avoidance of stating our opinions. The same is true with Joe.

We're also genuinely complimentary to one another. It's like a successful marriage. On the program we aim to make each other look good, to rescue the other from awkwardness or foot-in-mouth disease. Hugh and I especially have a team feeling about our joint interviews, picking up almost imperceptible cues from one another that we want to ask the next question or pass the ball.

Nor are we jealous of each other's triumphs. There is a generosity of spirit. There is also the conviction that as we, individually, become more adept at our work and more important to the public, the whole program becomes more important. As Joe Garagiola puts it, "There's no such thing as a good Amos and a bad Andy."

There's a final element: although I can't imagine being fonder of any two men, I know little of their day-to-day personal or social life. We talk about personalities and news events and our work, but our private lives remain essentially private. I think most working relationships could benefit by excluding personal matters from the office chatter.

In view of this, it does make me laugh sometimes when viewers write in to speculate about romances between us. The letters run the gamut from, "We know what you and Hugh are doing with your hands under the desk," to "It's becoming obvious that the three of you really dislike each other."

While I'm against office flirtations, under the desk or otherwise, I'm all for flirting at almost all other occasions. I love to flirt, and to be flirted with. One of my favorite interviews was with the actor Oskar Werner. I began on the air by commenting that I had read that he was a very difficult person. He gazed at me with luxuriant sleepiness for a moment and then asked softly, "But how do you know? We've never had an affair." I forget how the rest of the interview went.

The author Lawrence Durrell also registers sensuality, Yves Montand burns with it, and Richard Burton looks at every woman who interests him as though her clothes were slipping off.

It's interesting to me that all of these sexy-seeming men are European; I think most American men tend to treat a woman as a pal for jogging. European men usually give the impression they have something else in mind. Dr. Benjamin Spock describes this as sexual recognition, rather than sexual advance.

He writes, "Americans are presumably as sexually competent in the bedroom as any other group. But what is under discussion here is something more subtle and apparently more difficult to attain: sufficient sexual and romantic maturity to allow a person—man or woman—to show, whenever he is dealing with a member of the opposite sex, that he is pleasantly aware of this and that he can be appropriately attentive and charming, without implying an intention of further seductiveness."

Perhaps Americans are afraid of really being taken seriously if they flirt a little. Men worry that they'll have a drink dumped on their heads and women that they'll be considered promiscuous. Actually a man or woman who is *really* on the hunt is unmistakable; there's an edge of desperation that can't be hidden. To quote Louis Armstrong's famous answer when he was asked to describe jazz, "If you don't know it, I can't tell you."

Besides, real sexuality isn't eroticism alone. All the best qualities go into that kind of an aura, like humor, health, generosity, warmth, and even intelligence. I once received a thank-you note from Joshua Logan after a *Today* interview and it pleased me so much because it said, "You are a lady as well as a sexy woman, and part of that sex is your brains." I'd never known until then that I had sexy brains.

One of the happiest examples I know of lighthearted flirtation is the contented married author who ten years ago assured an equally contented married woman that they should run away together, in a balloon. His application for a balloon permit is safely tied up in red tape by civil aeronautical authorities in two countries, but he gives her progress reports whenever they turn up at the same party.

As I write this, I think of Mrs. Sargent Shriver telling me of her flirtation with of all people President Charles de Gaulle. When her husband was our Ambassador to France, Mrs. Shriver, the former Eunice Kennedy, was seated next to President de Gaulle at a formal state dinner. Mrs. Shriver said that she expected to find De Gaulle exact and formidable. Instead he was warm and funny and so interested in her that at the end of the dinner she said, "Mr. President, my only regret is that you are not twenty years younger and that I am not twenty years younger."

She later repeated this conversation to Madame de Gaulle, who replied with unexpected humor, "Ah yes, Mrs. Shriver, but just remember, I would then also be twenty years younger."

Which reminds me that it is a compliment too when someone flirts with your husband. I arrived at this generous conclusion just recently when Barbara Howar, a well-known Washington hostess and blossoming television personality, informed me cheerily that since she met my husband, she had stopped wanting my job. She now wanted my husband. When she told us, both Lee and I beamed.

That's general flirting-for-fun, but every now and then you meet a new man who makes you want to play the game for real. What can you do to make him want you?

Nothing on earth, if he isn't ready. Psychologists who make pronouncements about why and how people become infatuated with one another agree that one of the essential factors is availability. If he's in love with someone else, he's a brick wall as far as you are concerned and you're wasting your time sloshing on the perfume and telling him that he's the image of Steve McQueen.

If, however, he is something less than insanely in love with another woman, you are a contender. So first of all, stand back and assess him. Is he a quiet man who would be most comfortable with ladylike behavior, or would he like to be teased and shook up a bit? How does he see himself, as a man of dignity, an eccentric, a sage?

Don't make the adolescent mistake of trying to impress a man by insulting him. It doesn't demonstrate that you're hard to get, just hard to like. It seems to me that, Women's Liberation Movement aside, women come on awfully strong these days and men are unhappy about it. A college lecturer told me he was amazed at the applause, cheering and stamping from the young men in his audience when he criticized the aggressiveness of the modern woman. I agree with some of what the new feminists are saying, but I think they're way off in trying to change the biological roles as they apply to the sexes. Why spoil all the fun?

It's terribly old-fashioned of me, I know, but I still feel that a woman who wants to win a man should allow him the initiative. Her best bet is to concentrate on making him want it. To this end, nothing is more beguiling in this age of kooks and neurotics than the sunniness of a good mood. A look of wholeness is a distinct joy, not to mention a distinct novelty.

So don't tell him what your psychiatrist said, and what happened when you ran into your first husband last week, or about the office bitch who is after your job.

And don't insist that you don't want to be married, not ever, never, *never*. A lot of women calculate that's what men want to hear, so they pour on the bliss of singleness in order to reduce male anxiety. It has the opposite effect —the lady protests too much.

In fact, don't talk excessively about yourself at all in the beginning. Even if you're an older woman and unmarried, it doesn't require an explanation. These days some smashingly attractive women are marrying for the

144

first time in their forties or even fifties—I'm thinking of Geraldine Stutz, president of Henri Bendel, or Pauline Frederick, NBC's correspondent at the United Nations. Both married after the age of forty. And a great many women aren't marrying at all, out of choice—theirs.

In the first flush of youth, a man may marry a girl because he is attracted to her and she's pretty, but as he grows older, especially if his first marriage failed, he looks for more enduring qualities in the woman he will marry: good disposition, even temperament, and something as simple as tenacity.

The director and acting teacher Lee Strasberg recently married again. His wife is a young woman, a former pupil. I asked him how he happened to choose her, of all the women he knows. He smiled as he replied, "I could see the first act, and as I am a director I was able to imagine what the second act will be like, and the third."

So take it easy on the personal confessions. It will come out as time goes by, when the relationship is well enough established that the skeletons in the closet will be considered amusing decor. Project warmth: it's in short supply.

There's a great line in the play *Harvey* that fits here. Elwood P. Dowd is asked, "God, man, haven't you any righteous indignation?"

He replies: "Dr. Chumley, my mother used to say to me, 'In this world, Elwood'—she always called me Elwood—she'd say, 'In this world, Elwood, you must be oh, so smart or oh, so pleasant.' For years I was smart. I recommend pleasant. You may quote me."

I have.

9
Parties

The origin of a modern party is anthropological: humans meet and share food to lower hostility between them and indicate friendship. It's a fine, commendable idea. But the ritual achieves its most hectic and heroic form in the North American at-home dinner party.

Europeans rarely invite friends to their homes, which they consider to be sanctuaries, but prefer to entertain in restaurants. Americans think it is more gracious to go to the considerable trouble of eating and drinking under their own roofs. There's a high compliment involved in welcoming people to your home. It's your castle, even if it's one room, and it means a lot that you are willing to share it.

But your good intentions will count for nothing if you haven't put thoughtful preparation into your party. Being a hostess is about the hardest work there is, whether the party is a success or not; better to be exhausted and happy than exhausted and contemplating suicide.

Rule One: Never take on more than you can handle. Don't plan such an elaborate party that you are frazzled before it begins; don't have a menu that requires you to shuttle into the kitchen all night long; don't throw a cocktail party so big the guests are vertical sardines; don't blow the party budget on one lavish item, like filet mignon, so that you have to serve it in stingy amounts with a third-rate wine.

Rule Two: Get your party in focus—why are you giving it? If you have a guest of honor in mind, a visiting celebrity or a newly promoted executive, would he rather attend a large, impersonal cocktail party where he'll meet and be seen by many people, or a small intimate dinner where good conversation is more possible? The latter is more personal and flattering, but it places a heavy responsibility on the hostess to assemble guests who will hit it off with each other and with the guest of honor.

Personally I prefer dinner parties. Large cocktail parties are an infamous technique for ridding yourself of social obligations to people you usually don't know well or like much, which is such an unpromising beginning that I've rarely known one that recovered and turned into a great party.

Rule Three: Study your facilities. Your kitchen and freezer can cope with an overload, within reason; beyond that lies disaster. The size of your dining room might seem to limit the number of guests you can have but there are ingenious methods of extending this restriction.

148

Before Lee and I were married, I gave a birthday party for him in my three-room apartment and set up tables in the bedroom. A cooperative neighbor let me store my bedroom furniture in her apartment and I rented two round tables and covered them with rented cloths that went to the floor. Another rented cloth covered my bureau, converting it into a serving table. It couldn't have worked better, especially as we were able to return to an uncluttered living room when we finished eating. (And you will note, please, that he did marry me.)

But sometimes it is necessary to have a party as large as you can manage. This happens when the guest wants to meet a great many people, perhaps because he is running for political office, or when a great many people want to meet the guest, as when you're giving the reception after the symphony for a visiting soprano. In that case, either leave the food and drink preparation and serving to the professionals or keep the menu very simple—casserole, salad, cake, and coffee. You can demonstrate the personal touch in your flower arrangements or ingenuity in the décor.

If you live in an area, as I do, where flowers are very expensive, substitute scented candles. They give a lovely light with a hint of perfume or spice, and can be used again and again. Use candles at dinner to make all the women look beautiful, dispensing with electric light if you can; but don't have the dining room so dark that the guests have to grope for the salt and pepper. Also you might try a lighting expert's technique and put pink bulbs in your lamps. They flatter every face.

If you think you have problems, imagine the ones faced by those responsible for planning state dinners at the

White House. Bess Abell, who was White House social secretary during the Johnson years, told me that it was like putting together "a giant jigsaw puzzle."

"It's gathering together the pieces of the guest list; it's making that fit with the things that the foreign visitor wants to see and do while he's in this country; it's planning the entertainment—something that he will enjoy; it's getting the stage up; it's gathering together the Marine Band; working with the men in the floor room, getting the flowers on the table; and it's all the bits and pieces that make up an exciting, beautiful, glamorous party."

It's also knowing about food, Bess told the *Today* audience. In case there is some delay on sitting down to the table, the White House fish course is always something in a sauce that can stay hot; soufflés, and all other dishes that can't wait, are out of the question.

White House dinners make use of round tables seating ten each and scatter the VIPs one to a table, eliminating the pecking-order method of seating dignitaries down from the salt. Thomas Jefferson introduced round dining tables to the White House and people have admired them ever since for the opportunity they provide for general conversations. You can have round tables at your party too by renting them—either the whole table or else round tops to put on your own tables.

Mrs. Jacob Javits has two round tables constantly set up in her dining room, instead of one long rectangular size. In my dining room, I have a round table too. Mine seats as many as ten. It is a very inexpensive table but no one sees that as it is covered with a long cloth to the floor, which matches the material on my walls and my draperies. If I'm having a large party seating more than ten people,

I open up a folding round table and cover it with a cloth identical to the one always on display.

But even the most experienced hostess sometimes falters. Bess Abell also told me about a White House near-disaster when her party planning came close to straining diplomatic relations with Britain. Harold Wilson was to be a dinner guest and Bess invited a White House favorite, Robert Merrill, to sing. Merrill's choice of songs arrived a few days later and was sent to be printed in the program. The President's aide, Walt Rostow, called Bess in anguish. "You can't be serious," he groaned. "You really *can't* be serious."

Merrill innocently had selected *On the Road to Mandalay,* that grand old colonializing song, at a time when the British forces east of the Suez had just been withdrawn, and *I Got Plenty of Nothin'*—and Britain had just devalued the pound. Merrill saved the situation by adding an encore, *It Ain't Necessarily So.*

BUFFETS

A buffet dinner is the easiest of all parties to give, but it has its hazards. Some people always give buffet parties—Lauren Bacall is one who comes to mind—and through experience they go so smoothly that they look effortless. They're not.

The lack of structure can work adversely. Sometimes a guest turns away from the buffet with his plate full and his courage empty because there isn't a group he feels assured enough to join. Or else, as happened to me one time, I was among the first in line at the buffet and then sat at a table alone for what seemed an endless length of time while the other guests seated themselves elsewhere. I kept telling myself it wasn't personal. I even whispered, "I am the way I am, I look the way I look. I am my age."

At a small buffet, place cards are the best answer to avoid this situation. A sit-down buffet can be as elegant as a formal dinner—the guest serves himself and then sits down at an already set table, where his place card indicates. It's a good idea in such circumstances to check ahead of time whom you'll be sitting with, so that you all go to the buffet at about the same time.

Place cards can be effective icebreakers, too. I sometimes use dime-store clues instead of place cards—a pair of doll's sunglasses for an actress on her way to California, a toy camera for a photographer, needle and thread for a designer. People unerringly find their assigned places and have a good time doing it.

Place cards don't have to be elaborate; Senator and Mrs. Jacob Javits have used cards crayoned by their children.

Somewhat larger buffets—anywhere from twelve to fifty people—are even easier than the ones with place settings. First of all, the hostess never has to worry about there being more men than women or the reverse, and who should be sitting with whom. Guests take their laden plates to small stacked tables that have been scattered about, or to the coffee table, or any place else they can put down wineglass and plate. At informal parties, guests cheerfully sit on the floor. Just make certain that there is room for everyone to sit and put his plate somewhere; no one likes to stand to eat.

Buffets also lend themselves to ingenious menu ideas—the only restriction is that the knife must not be required, fork food only. Barbara Howar, who gives the best informal parties in Washington, gave a party for me where the guests served themselves soul food in her kitchen and sat on the floor to eat it. She passed around brownies afterward as dessert. It couldn't have been more casual and the guests couldn't have been more impressive—they included Presidential aide Henry Kissinger, former Secretary for Health, Education and Welfare Robert Finch, Senator George McGovern, and Art Buchwald.

Another time when Barbara was entertaining, she simply sent out for Chinese food.

Nancy Martin, wife of Ernest Martin of the Feuer and Martin producing team, loves casual Sunday night parties. A favorite menu: chili, salad, apple pie.

I recently had a party in my not-very-large apartment for fifty people. I must confess that our toddler spent the night with my mother, and we set up tables in her room and every other usable room. I served paella (making sure that all the chicken was off the bones), salad, and a choice of cheesecake and chocolate fudge cake.

I don't entertain very often, but I think the best party menu I ever had was the time we served pot roast, potato pancakes, apple sauce and a huge pot of stuffed cabbage that my mother made. Our guests that night included Carol Channing, Alan King, and Senator Javits, who said it was the best dinner he had eaten in months. He also wondered if mother was available for private parties. She was so pleased, she almost said "Yes." The point is you should serve what comes easiest and what you do best. Don't worry about how elegant or impressive your menu is. One actress I know gave an after-theater buffet and served marvelous oversized hotdogs, with all the trimmings, and ice cold beer. The famous Richard Rodgers' Christmas Eve Party always features the "omelette man," Rudolph Stanish, who arrives complete with omelette batter and prepares your serving whenever you're ready, folding it over a choice of fillings that include creamed chicken, or sour cream and red caviar, or bacon and chopped parsley. Each one takes him about fifteen seconds to make, a showstopper in itself.

Richard and Dorothy Rodgers have streamlined the table arrangements too. The dining room is filled with small tables set with decorations and wineglasses. You bring with you from the buffet your omelette, silver, and napkin. When you finish eating, the table is quickly cleared and a fresh wineglass put in place ready for the next guest. It's a system that allows a large number of people to eat in comfort.

Crepes are another good buffet idea. They can be made in advance—my husband is a splendid crepe-maker—and a variety of fillings offered. Curries are good too, because the extras can be imaginative.

FORMAL DINNERS

The formal dinner party is more impressive, but it is vastly more difficult not only because it requires so much serving and plate removing but also because it is vulnerable to the whims or health of the guests. Whether you've invited twelve or twenty, or two, last-minute additions or subtractions ruin the symmetry. We have friends who like to entertain twenty and always invite twenty-two, assuming a normal loss of one couple. The last time we were guests there, all twenty-two made it; the host and hostess didn't sit down with us.

154

Mrs. Irving Stone, wife of the author, heard of the New York hostess' trick of inviting twenty-two to get twenty and was astonished. In California, she says, if you want twenty dinner guests you invite ten: "It will expand on its own."

THE GUEST LIST

Homogeneity is much to be admired—in milk, for instance—but not for parties. If you're entertaining in honor of a banker, don't invite wall-to-wall bankers and financiers. They see one another every working day and would welcome a change.

Unless it is a sentimental occasion, such as an anniversary, mix in a few new people even when you're inviting the gang. Interesting people are always an asset whatever the professions or whether or not they've met the other guests before.

Give some consideration to the human chemistry of your party. You'll want several talkers, so make certain that there are also some listeners available. If the group is likely to be low-keyed, mix in some who are spirited. Add an unexpected element just as cooks do, for flavor.

Mollie Parnis, the dress designer, is a hostess with striking ideas about combinations of people. When I interviewed the ex-Secretary of State Dean Rusk, Mollie promptly began to plan a party for him. "I think he'd enjoy meeting Mia Farrow," she told me. I don't know if he would or not, but I'm sure the other guests would have enjoyed seeing them meet.

That's typical of a Mollie Parnis party. She's designed

clothes worn by Mamie Eisenhower, Lady Bird Johnson, and Muriel Humphrey, as well as the rich and famous from both the social world and showbusiness, so her guest list is exotic. She will give a party for Kirk and Anne Douglas and invite twenty people they've never met. She'll put together instead a *New York Times* editor, or Martin Gabel and his wife Arlene Francis, or Richard Feigen, who owns a prestigious art gallery, and his wife Sondra, or Leonard and Sylvia Lyons, and some doctors, lawyers, and Wall Street bankers. The point is that she doesn't concern herself with what people do or if they're old pals—she's after color and texture, the same qualities that make her clothes outstanding.

THE INVITATIONS

There are some aids to make life easier here, too. Whether you send out written invitations or call guests on the phone, give them an idea of what kind of dress is expected for your party. A dinner party we gave recently stipulated "informal" so the men knew that black tie wouldn't be worn, and the women knew that they could wear anything. Some arrived in midi dresses, several in pants suits, one in a snakeskin poncho; I wore short organza.

If you want your party to be more formal in tone, suggest dark suits for the men, cocktail dresses for women. On really informal occasions, you might write or say "Dress in your own style." Personally, I hate the overdirected party . . . costume parties or those cutesy-poo affairs where guests are instructed to dress as someone they wish they

156

were. I'd dress like someone who wished she hadn't been invited in the first place.

Every now and then, parties pose a tricky problem that can be best handled by an adroitly worded invitation. I'm thinking in particular of the party we gave for Hugh and Ruth Downs on their silver wedding anniversary. The Downses live in Arizona now and keep a New York apartment that is too small for large-scale entertaining, so Lee and I decided to have a party for them.

I asked the Downses for a guest list and they gave me about twenty names, most of whom were high-ranking NBC executives who are also personal friends of the Downses—the chairman of the board, for instance; the president of the network, the executive vice-president, the producer of our *Today* show and so on. I, worried (a) that my friends would wonder why *they* hadn't been asked to the party, and (b) that the NBC brass might think I was using the event to advance my own career.

The solution lay in the wording of the invitations. I wrote on my personal stationery: *Hugh and Ruth Downs have asked us to invite you to a party on the occasion of their twenty-fifth wedding anniversary. We hope you can come* . . . and then I gave the particulars of time, place, and dress.

SEATING ARRANGEMENTS

When there are place cards or when you are in control of the seating, my rule of thumb is to place someone he knows on one side of the guest and someone he doesn't know on the other. I also try to alternate listeners and talkers to

157

some extent, but I have no patience with that old saw about widely separating husbands and wives. In fact, at a dinner party where many people are strangers, I think it eases the flutters to put husbands and wives at the same table. I do agree, though, that they shouldn't be placed side by side; it has a Noah's Ark look.

And I love the story about the blasé young model who married a titled, aged Englishman and sighed in relief, "Thank God, now we no longer have to sit together at dinner parties."

I watched Pat Nixon handle a complicated seating problem at a White House luncheon for press ladies. We knew about the tables for ten and all of us were wondering which nine of us would sit down with her. Her diplomatic maneuver was simplicity: she placed her co-hosts, wives of cabinet ministers, one to a table and then asked all the press ladies to join her in drawing lots to discover where we would sit. It's almost impossible to please the suspicious ladies of the press. That day, Mrs. Nixon succeeded.

RECEIVING LINES?

Even in these times of relaxed, if not extinct, etiquette, there is something to be said for preserving the receiving line. I remember when I reported on the wedding of Julie Nixon to David Eisenhower, the families had intended to dispense with the receiving line for the sake of informality. But it was soon discovered that there was no other way to make certain that every guest was greeted.

Even small parties need an informal "receiving line"— the host or hostess standing near the door to welcome guests—and it becomes imperative at large cocktail parties where newcomers may come and go without meeting a soul or laying eyes on the host or hostess. During the first hour of a party, *you* are what it takes to make the person glad he came.

At a very stately affair, your name will be announced thunderously as you start down the receiving line. Otherwise, when you must go through a formal receiving line and don't know all the people in it, introduce yourself, say something about yourself if it's pertinent; say you're happy to be there, or the wedding was beautiful, but don't dally and hold up the line.

INTRODUCTIONS

I often wish name tags were acceptable at parties, with terse information under the name such as: John Roadhouse, *Rich Bigot*, or Suzie Walker, *Feminist!*

Failing this, the responsibility for helping people identify one another falls upon the hosts. The rule books say in general to introduce the man to the woman. Don't introduce people merely by name alone. Since you know something about them both, your introduction can serve as a catalyst. It's easiest when people have interesting jobs, and you can say, "This is George Bigelow, who is doing all those fascinating heart transplants," or "This is Esther Morris, the new buyer in the jewelry department."

If you're introducing guests who can't be identified by occupation, give them other kinds of clues about one another. "This is Joyce Harvey, who has become an avid cyclist lately, and this is Bob Scherer, who just moved to

159

town." Then they both have some idea of how they can get a conversation going as you drift away.

However, as *The New Yorker* magazine says, don't editorialize—just give the news. Don't make every introduction a rave: it can cause much more embarrassment than pleasure. I dread lyrical introductions of me, studded with gooey "marvelous on the *Today* show, you must have heard of her," when I can see by the stranger's expression that he never heard of me or the *Today* show.

Occasionally you will introduce people who, unbeknown to you, have been mutually involved in some bitter marital breakdown. Try to separate them discreetly but don't agonize if you can't. And don't hand-wring and apologize all evening long. If either one is too insensate to tolerate being in the same room with the other, it is his duty as a guest to leave. Given all of space in which to roam, galaxies collide; it's no one's fault when two people meet accidentally and sizzle.

Except when it is a *very* large party, everyone should be introduced. You can sometimes facilitate the job by guiding newcomers around the room in small bunches of two or three, but you should try to overlook no one. Don't hesitate because you don't like to disturb a congenial group and require the men to stand. The temporary nuisance of it doesn't justify having a guest feel awkward and slighted all evening because there are some people he hasn't met.

THE PARTY'S UNDERWAY

You can settle down, but don't get into long conversations. You've got work to do, watching for people marooned in silence on the fringes of the party. Don't be too obvious when going to the rescue. If you obviously drag the wallflower into the nearest animated group, his pride will be singed. Join him casually and find something to talk about. You're the hostess and sooner or later someone will join you, allowing you to slip away.

If you're having a formal dinner and want to get things rolling, making the guests feel relaxed and involved, consider the ancient custom of proposing toasts. And don't worry about making the perfect speech. Toasts can be and, most often, are fun. More than one toast is perfectly O.K. too. My husband led off at the anniversary party we gave for Hugh and Ruth Downs and invited me to be next. It became contagious and everyone proposed a toast to the Downses, including the Downses.

I also admire the European custom of separating the sexes for about twenty minutes after a sit-down dinner. One hostess I know always asks the ladies to "repair" to her bedroom to freshen their make-up and chat, while the men have brandy and cigars in the den. I thought it terribly old-fashioned the first time we all trooped behind her, but I soon saw why it is a very practical idea. It gives women a chance to fix their faces leisurely and get to know each other better, as women invariably do when men aren't present. And it gives the men a chance to swap the jokes that their wives don't think are at all funny.

CHILDREN

Small children do not belong at an adult party, and especially should not be used like trained midgets to help

161

serve martinis. Around the age of eight, if they have social aplomb, they can help at the door to show guests where coats are kept. In this case they should be introduced, by their full names, and they should be prepared to respond courteously. Once the party has begun, children should vanish. Under no circumstances should children be asked to sing or otherwise perform for guests who aren't members of the family.

I make a small sentimental exception in the case of new babies or very tiny children. Proud parents can tote them around the room and show them off, providing it's done fairly quickly and isn't repeated.

AFTER THE BALL IS OVER

When guests depart, the same personal contact extended when they arrived is expected. If, as so often happens, the guests leave all at once like an avalanche, the host and hostess should disentangle themselves from whatever else they were doing and post themselves near the door to say goodnight. The final goodbyes and drive safelys round off the point that the party is supposed to make—that the guests are all people you like very much.

Don't make it difficult for departing guests to leave by protesting that it's still early, or "You *can't* go so soon!" If it's a week night, most of the guests will have to get up early the next morning. As a person who rises long before dawn, I know I'm grateful to hosts who allow me to slip away without having to explain and apologize more than once.

The guests who won't go pose another kind of problem.

Obviously they're having a good time, which is a credit to your hospitality, but enough's enough. It sometimes helps to stop serving liquor, but if this doesn't work simply be frank. Try something like, "I've loved having you here, and I'm mad about all of you, but I'm suddenly so sleepy I can't keep my eyes open. You can stay if you like, but I may start to snore"; or simply, "I wish it weren't so late— I wish the party were just begnining—but the fact is that we have to be up early tomorrow morning."

I know one celebrated host who just goes to bed when he's ready. Eventually the guests notice his absence and get the hint. Another used to put a recording of Oriental music on the record player, turn up the volume and announce beamingly to startled guests, "This is my room-emptying music." They would laugh, gather up their coats good-humoredly, and leave.

YOU, THE PERFECT GUEST

We tell children as they set off to their first parties, "Be sure and thank the hostess, and *don't fight!*" The philosophy works for adult parties too. When you're a guest you have an obligation to make the hostess believe you're having a good time, which involves more than the thank-you note or telephone call the next day. You behave during the party as though you're glad you came. If you aren't feeling well you conceal it, or leave; if you're despondent, you wear a smile anyway; if you're shy, you make an effort to mix in spite of it.

You don't fight, of course, but you don't have to be superficial and avoid any clash of ideas. So long as you

163

aren't insulting or vicious, you can dispute another guest's opinion. But you can't dominate the party with a running debate and passion is no excuse for losing control of yourself.

Contribute to the party by taking on some of the hostess' role. If she isn't around to make the introductions right away, introduce yourself. Give your full name and some helpful indication of who you are. Don't sit back waiting to be amused: bring along some conversation starters as a sort of quiet hostess gift and be alert to possible subject matter in an idle reference someone else may make. Help make the party go—you'll have a better time, too.

And when you thank the hostess, don't generalize vaguely about "lovely party." Compliment her on something specific: the flowers, the unusual canapés, how unruffled and beautiful she managed to look throughout, the chocolate mousse she made that was the best dessert you ever tasted.

Don't overlook the host. Tell him you've never felt so pampered, or never had such a stimulating evening. Tell him he's been so interesting you'd like to run away with him; tell him to be sure when you do to bring the recipe for the chocolate mousse.

AFTER THE PARTY

If you know the hostess well, telephone the next morning, not too early. Otherwise send a thank-you note, or some variation of it. Instead of sending the usual flowers, Eleanor and Frank Perry sent our daughter a toy after they had been dinner guests at our home. Arlene and Martin Gabel sent a huge jar of jellybeans with the label, *To the Gubers, Thank You.* Geraldine Stutz sends a thank-you telegram right after she leaves a party.

If you think a small gift is indicated, you might send some cookies or fudge or jelly you've made yourself. Flowers are fine, but even though they are proper after a party, I personally prefer to receive them before the party so everyone can enjoy them.

And be firm with yourself; don't procrastinate. If you delay a few days, your thanks will lose that first bloom of sincerity and seem more like the performance of a tiresome duty.

10

The Lecturer Comes To Town

It's a traveling time. International names can be found in motels that sprawl outside small American cities, and even hamlets boast a lecturer with a front-page face. Causes think of fund-raising in terms of a famous person: in Connecticut the California grape boycott committee wonders if Paul Newman will host a benefit, in black ghettos the free breakfast group speculates about Harry Belafonte. Service clubs plan their annual conventions around the availability of glamorous names, to draw the delegates, and actors take to the road to plug their new movie, or a politician.

There's so much movement, in fact, that by all the laws of chance there is every likelihood that you'll be spending some time with a visiting celebrity, and a strong possibility that you may be required to make the arrangements for his care and feeding.

Big celebrities either cost a lot of money, or come for free; there's nothing in between. They come free to help something they believe in, usually when someone they trust has assured them that it's genuine. Otherwise they

167

charge well into four figures but they are a blue-chip investment; subscriptions to lecture series are relatively easy to sell and hugely profitable.

In Dayton, Ohio, for instance, a lecture series is booked into an auditorium that holds two thousand people—and each lecturer must speak three times because the series has sold six thousand tickets. I estimate that a season like that one can earn about fifty thousand dollars clear for whatever charity the ladies have in mind.

Lecturers can vary from your local police chief to J. Edgar Hoover or the Attorney General of the United States, who address important meetings concerned with criminology. Dress designers like Bill Blass are available, or an authority on antiques, or authors, or even titled Englishmen like the delightful Duke of Bedford or Lord Harlech, who was lecturing when his frequent date married Aristotle Onassis.

Kitty Carlisle loves to lecture, Bennett Cerf averages one a month, Bess Myerson and Hildegarde are popular on the circuit and so are former athletes like Phil Rizzuto and my colleague from the *Today* show, Joe Garagiola. Composer Richard Adler, who wrote *Pajama Game* and *Damn Yankees*, plays his songs and tells stories about Presidents he has entertained.

With many, the money is a happy incidental: they plain love to lecture. Bennett Cerf disarmingly admits that he likes the attention he receives. In my case I enjoy lecturing because the women I meet are so intelligent and well-informed that I am protected against my New Yorker's vision of America—that it ends at the Hudson River.

It's best to contact a lecture bureau. Very few celebrities book their own lectures on a free-lance basis, and it's time-wasting trying to locate them. You'll discover when you inquire that the lecture comes at a flat fee whether you have an audience of two hundred in mind or two thousand. You're paying for the lecturer's time, rather than on a sliding scale according to the number of warm bodies you can assemble.

Generally, the fee covers the lecturer's expenses; special arrangements must be made if the lecturer comes a long distance just for one speech, and has no others in the vicinity.

Both parties sign a contract, which protects the audience against the lecturer not turning up. If the lecturer can't make it for a very good reason, the bureau sends someone of equal calibre.

Most lecturers are linked with a topic in the brochure but some, people who are in news-making, adjust their subject matter to suit recent events or the special interest of the group they are addressing.

WHAT'S INVOLVED

Three things, usually. There is a question period after the speech, an autograph session after that, and a meal. Sometimes a small group, the sponsoring club's executive or the leading members of the campus faculty, host the lecturer at a luncheon or dinner just before the speech or immediately following; sometimes the event is a luncheon or dinner speech, attended by the entire lecture audience.

Ahead of time, confirm the topic and read whatever press clippings you can find in order to guess the effectiveness of the speaker. Your enthusiasm will influence ticket sales, if you haven't a sold-out subscription. Write for press photos and a biography, which you will relay to your local newspaper; notify radio and television stations of his expected arrival.

If the celebrity is very important or a home-town boy or from your state, invite the mayor or even the governor to attend.

As the time draws nearer, check on the arrangements for accommodation. Usually the lecturer arrives the night before the speech and makes his reservation himself in a local hotel. Confirm that there is no mix-up. If the lecturer has left the reservation to you, and you are paying his expenses, it's a lovely gesture to make him feel important by booking him a suite rather than a room. Sometimes the hotel will give you a break on the cost, in return for the prestige and publicity of having such a famous guest, but don't promise in exchange to have him pose with the manager.

There's nothing more thoughtful than putting flowers in the room, or something to eat or drink if the celebrity is likely to arrive after room service has been discontinued. I was made to feel so cared for late one night when I checked into a strange hotel to find waiting in my room some home-made cookies, cakes and fruit, and a small bottle of chilled wine.

Another speaker I know, who arrived somewhat incredulously in the small Canadian city of Medicine Hat, was greeted by three red roses from the lady deputy mayor. Some lecture sponsors regularly put fruit, cheese, biscuits and chocolate in the guest's room.

Some speakers, including me, Selma Diamond and Helen Gurley Brown, would rather not be met at the airport; it's more restful to come into town on our own. I gather, however, that we are exceptions: most lecturers prefer to put themselves immediately in the hands of greeting hosts to enable them to get the feel of the city and learn something about it well in advance of the speech.

You establish this preference ahead of time, of course. If the guest would rather not be met, supply a limousine with a driver who can spot the guest as he or she gets off the plane and take over the chore of collecting the luggage.

If the celebrity wants to be met, and time provides, do some homework beforehand and discover his interests. Dorothy Rodgers fondly recalls a visit she and Richard made to St. Louis, where a couple met them at the airport and drove them to see some of the art museums and interesting houses—exactly what Dorothy most wanted to see.

If the celebrity has an empty evening during his scheduled visit, ask if he would like to be entertained; don't assume that he can't be bothered, or that he's already booked. Find out if he would like a small dinner party, or a large reception, and if he has friends in the community he'd like to see there.

I have especially warm memories of a hostess in Jackson, Michigan, who left a note for me to find when I arrived at the hotel the night before my lecture. The note invited me to what she described as a small dinner party. It went on to tell me that there would be ten guests, who some of the guests were and that I would be home by ten. My hostess said that she would love for me to come but would understand if I were too tired. Usually strange dinner parties are more fatiguing than relaxing, but here I was given as many of the facts as possible. The evening sounded intimate, interesting and I would be home early. I accepted with anticipation and had a wonderful time.

Don't be offended if the celebrity would rather be alone. It does take an effort to be continuously charming and full of vitality, and there's an emotional and physical drain in jet travel as well. If he feels it's wiser to save his energy for the lecture, don't press him to change his mind.

A detail that can become a nightmare: Double-check the itinerary and airline reservation. It's easy to make a mistake on the flight time or even the date, and thoroughly wreck the celebrity's disposition.

Some celebrities prefer to travel with a friend or relative, not only for the company they provide but also to act as a buffer between themselves and the possible rudeness of strangers who recognize them, and, if they are alone, feel free to join them for a chat. Women lecturers, I think, are especially vulnerable and forlorn when traveling alone. I know one experienced woman reporter who always over-tips when she arrives in a strange city. She explains, "I buy kindness."

While we're on the subject of travel: Very often a lecture committee makes great plans to meet the speaker at the airport when she arrives and to take her with speed to the lecture hall, but they forget about her after the lecture.

Do make certain that there is transportation for your speaker when she wants to go back to the airport to return home.

Don't make any commitments for press interviews or radio and television appearances without checking first with the guest. Some celebrities love a schedule crammed with interviews: it's an ego-stroking way to pass the time and gives them an opportunity to plug whatever book, picture or cause they choose. Others feel it is an imposition.

If he agrees to whatever you can line up, make it as easy as possible. Schedule newspaper and radio tape interviews together or consecutively and have a car to take him to studio appointments. Avoid delivering him long before he is actually required in front of the camera or microphone. It's tiresome and a mood-dropper to spend an hour sipping machine coffee, talking to receptionists, and producers who pop in every fifteen minutes and promise, "We're almost ready!"

THE QUESTION PERIOD

The question period is becoming a standard feature of the lecture routine. On some campuses, in fact, when radicals, politicians or authors with a strong point of view are scheduled to speak, the speech itself is merely a prelude to the questions.

Even speakers with such non-controversial topics as interior decoration can expect to be asked to allow a short

173

time for questions. It gives the audience a sense of participation and an outlet for frustration if he disagrees with the speaker.

When the audience is very large, the question period becomes almost impossible. I've seen it work in large theaters when traveling microphones are available, with spotters who watch for upraised hands and help the chairman sort out the priorities. If the speech concerns something crackling such as a zoning change or our foreign policy, it's worth all the trouble in order to allow a dialogue between speaker and audience. But otherwise it is unwieldy to invite questions from a huge crowd.

With a hot topic, watch out for the amateur orators, who are often superbly articulate and impassioned—but interminable. Announce ahead of time a fair cut-off point of, say, two minutes for each question. Hold a stopwatch and firmly instruct the questioner when his time is up that he must finish.

Few lecture circuit riders face audiences that are unruly. The problem with the question period, in fact, is usually that the ladies are too shy to get it started. Experienced program arrangers plant two or three questions with friends who have poise enough to get to their feet. And after a few of these, the entire audience grows bolder and there usually is a host of fluttering hands.

Another technique is the written questions. This doesn't work well in a large hall, but is a fine approach at the luncheon following the lecture, where the audience is considerably smaller. Have paper and pencils on the tables and explain that the questions will be collected during lunch. Most speakers like to see the questions in advance to weed out the duplications and, if they choose, the very personal questions. It's best if the speaker reads the question himself and then answers it, rather than involving another person.

The great Chicago hockey player Bobby Hull will sign autographs for hours, refusing offers of a police escort to get him out of a mob of fans. Other celebrities will sign none. You'll have to ask in advance how your guest feels about it. If he's plugging a book or a record, he may want you to help him arrange with the publisher or distributor to have copies available, so he can autograph these after the speech. Don't feel you have an obligation to help with this commercial venture. You can make it easy for him to sell his product if you like, but it's beyond your responsibility.

Some famous guests bring copies of their best photographs, already autographed, and distribute these after the speech. Jayne Mansfield had a unique variation of this—she gave away hot water bottles contoured like herself. (Fine for Jayne Mansfield but I wouldn't suggest it for Mia Farrow.)

Announce to the audience where autographs can be obtained—"at the back of the auditorium" or "in the hotel's Rose Room." Prepare the location with a desk or table and a chair, and make sure that there is ample space and good lighting. Suggest that the programs people are holding will be suitable for the souvenir autographs.

As a prudent bulwark against embarrassment, line up at least ten friends to start the move toward the autograph table. It's ghastly for the celebrity to sit there ignored, making nervous conversation with the committee about how hot or cold the weather has been.

THE BOOZE PROBLEM

Some lecturers are in the habit of bolstering their confidence with a drink or two before the speech, and a few are inclined to match their demand with the available supply. It isn't a good idea to schedule a long cocktail party before a speech. Through nervousness, the guest may not notice how much he is drinking until his eyes cross.

The lecture bureau, when asked discreetly, will advise you whether the speaker sticks to lemonade until after the speech, or prefers a nip. If drinks aren't going to be available before his speech, you might tell him about it so he can make his own arrangements before he arrives. On the other hand, if he's a leading churchman and doesn't drink, find out if he objects to the other guests being served liquor before the luncheon or dinner.

While you're asking the bureau the delicate question about drink, you can also check about the guest's food preferences. It's the height of thoughtfulness to provide him with a serving that fits his special diet, if he has one.

YOU'RE IN CHARGE

This is the year you're program convener so it's your job to greet the celebrity at the airport and be at his right hand until you return him to the plane. You're petrified, but you've got to go through with it.

Start affirmatively. Don't have a look of astonishment on your face as you say, "*You're* Barbara Walters!"—implying that there is a devastating gap between the vision on television and the frump in reality. Even if you're wrong ten times, continue to approach likely looking arriving passengers with a pleasant, smiling, "Aren't you Barbara Walters?"

It's a good idea not to use first names until you're invited to, no matter how familiar and folksy the celebrity may seem. Stars like Johnny Carson, whose face is known to a hundred million people, are put off by strangers who open up a conversation as though they have been friends for years.

If you've been selected to meet the celebrity because you've often remarked that you went to school together, give him a break by stating the situation right off. Say, "I'm certain you won't remember me, and there's no reason why you should, but I've been awfully proud to claim that we went to Miss Tissie's dancing class together when we were children."

When I told her I was writing this book, Jacqueline Susann gave me an example of the approach which is all too common. "The most horrible obstacle that befalls anyone who has made it is the non pro, a slob, who literally attacks you and grabs your shoulder and says, 'I bet you don't remember me.' Oh God! How many times I've longed to say, 'I certainly don't.'"

Jackie went on to say, "I hate my lingering traces of Philadelphia manners that causes me to manage a weak smile and say, 'Your face *is* familiar but . . .' Do they help you out? Not at all. He or she says, 'I'll give you a hint. Does the name Bessie Finer mean anything to you?' Of course it doesn't, but I say, 'It sounds familiar.'

"A triumphant smile appears and my shoulder is released. 'She sat next to you at Bryant School in Philadelphia. I'm her cousin.'

"Don't try and convince him that you *never* went to Bryant School. That only takes another hour and he gets belligerent, winds up saying you don't want to remember your old friends."

I knew exactly what Jacqueline Susann was talking about. There isn't a celebrity anywhere who hasn't endured a version of that little horror.

Don't let trivia fluster you. I've known airport greeters who kept everyone shivering in a blizzard while they sorted out who would sit in the back seat and who would sit in the front. Put the celebrity in the front beside the driver; it affords the best view and has slightly more prestige.

Conversation in the car between airport and hotel can be full of wretched silences and even more wretched banalities. You can make it easier to be comfortable with the celebrity if you start with practical matters, such as his schedule and whom he'll be meeting the next day. It's a master-stroke to provide him with a written timetable of the events that have been arranged and then verbally fill him in about the people he'll encounter. It's tactful to give him such information as, "The mayor's wife died recently," or "You'll be running into the president of our biggest industry and he likes to be treated with a big show of deference."

This is the time to go over the press arrangements and

warn the celebrity of interviewers who make a game of being abrasive.

Give him some of the highlights of your city: what it's proud of, what some of its problems are, what are most of its citizens talking about now. This will give him valuable material for starting conversations during his stay, for which he will be profoundly grateful to you.

Before you leave him at the hotel, verify his plans for the evening. If he intends to go on to a reception right away, wait in the lobby to take him. He'll appreciate a few minutes alone in his room to freshen up and make some phone calls.

On the way to the party, tell him something about the guests—the couple who have eleven children, the banker who plays golf at almost a professional level, the woman who just won a literary award. The guests will then not only be more interesting to him, but if he has a lively memory he'll be able to make a sensational impression by associating people with their achievement as he is introduced.

Ken McCormick, editor-in-chief at Doubleday, has an astounding faculty for this high flattery. Arthur Hailey, author of *Hotel* and *Airport*, once gave a party for Ken to introduce him to some thirty of his friends. Ken asked to be given some information about each, and Arthur obliged. Ken later met them all and, without a fluff, said to each, "Ah yes, you're the sportswriter," or "I hear you have the best-read column in the city."

If you're taking the celebrity to a restaurant to eat, and if you think he's particularly shy, arrange in advance for a secluded table so he will be able to eat his meal undisturbed. It's a nice touch, though, to suggest to the headwaiter that he can allow the captain or waiters or even the cook to say hello, if they wish.

Don't indicate that he's a dud by confiding that ticket sales have been slow. If you've really got a disaster on your hands, try to have the lecture moved to a small hall where the empty seats won't dominate with their gloom. If you can't move the event, tell the speaker, "We have such a huge ballroom—it's the only place available and we've never been able to fill it. So please don't be upset if you find there are only one hundred and fifty attending; that's all we ever sell."

Prepare him for all known eventualities. If you know the mothers of school-age children will have to leave at three o'clock whether the lecture is over or not, warn the speaker that they won't be leaving because of boredom. Caution him about the elderly ladies down front who usually nod off to sleep just as the talk is getting underway; tell him that it's nothing personal, they always do that because they're very elderly and the hall is usually warm.

Don't be demure about the length of time you want him to speak, effusing that the audience is just *dying* to listen for as long as he wants to go on. He's a professional and he can trim his goods to fit the situation. He'll be much less offended to learn that he has exactly forty minutes, because people must return to work, than to watch the room emptying long before he's reached his best material.

Try to provide the celebrity with a peaceful start in the morning. Call him to wake him up if he wants that and then leave him alone to get himself organized. In the case of a woman celebrity, and if it is possible, see if she would like the services of a hairdresser before she starts into the schedule. If time permits, perhaps the guest would like to tour some points of special interest in the city.

Keep in mind that you want him rested and in top form for the lecture, which is worth the sacrifice of a visit to the Diorama. A friend of mine in a Western city told me about the visits only six weeks apart of two famous and distinguished newscasters. Both were entertained at a luncheon before the lecture: the first one was bubbling with superlatives during the meal, loved the town, loved the people, couldn't bear to leave; the second, bone-tired, was so listless he could scarcely eat. It might have been better to allow the second man to sleep late that day, rather than hustle him around the town.

Just before the lecture, even normally communicative speakers are likely to fall silent and broody. You needn't worry that you've done something to offend. His mind is on the speech and he's thinking about his opening remarks, or a rearrangement of his material. Be still; he'll love you for it.

Your final responsibility is to get him to the airport on time. Sometimes this means cutting short the autograph session ruthlessly; you play the heavy, rather than putting the burden of disappointing people on him. Announce that it's possible for him to stay only a minute longer: "There's time for only three more autographs and then our guest must leave. He's been very kind, but we don't want him to miss his plane."

You can arrange for the autographs to be obtained by mail. Collect the books, albums, or programs, together with the names and addresses of disappointed fans. The celebrity can autograph them at his leisure and put them in the mail. Believe me, he'll be glad to—especially if book or record sales are involved.

Throughout the visit of the celebrity you're going to make some difficult decisions. Most of your friends will be expecting that you'll arrange for them to get to know the celebrity really well, by which they mean a long, earnest conversation about their ambitions to become a writer or their daughter's amazing talent that demands recognition. You're torn between enhancing your own social position and serving your function as a buttress between the celebrity and general nuisance.

It's a damned-if-you-do and damned-if-you-don't situation, particularly as many celebrities would resent being overprotected from people with a genuine interest in their work. It's best to consult with him as to the condition of his energy. If he says he's fresh out, you can tell your friends truthfully that he wasn't feeling up to meeting a great many people; if he's willing, allow access to him but advise people to be brief because others are anxious to talk to the celebrity as well. Lurk on the outskirts of the conversation, ready to catch his eye if he wants to be disentangled.

YOU'RE THE SPEAKER

If it hasn't happened yet, it soon will. Unless you're a total recluse, you can't avoid some public moment when you'll be obliged to introduce the guest speaker, or give a book report, or be spokesman for a delegation, or plug the forthcoming PTA Fun Fair on local television.

Mostly public speaking is an art you can only learn on

the job, and confidence will come with experience. In the meantime, however, there are tricks to help you through the novice period so that only your digestion will know what a strain it is.

The fundamental rule is preparation. Test pilots bullet into space with scarcely a heart flutter because they know their business; good public speakers, cheerily and effortlessly rambling on without a glance at their notes, have also done their homework—they've gone over and over the points they want to make, the structure of the speech, even the flourishes of humor.

You can get the best effect by emulating their example. Of all the methods of giving a speech, which include writing it all down and then reading it or else putting most of it on cards for near-constant reference, I much prefer learning the speech thoroughly—and then throwing it away.

Reading it from typed pages is a safe refuge for the scared, but unless you've taken drama lessons the words will be lead and the audience will stop listening. And I've seen inexperienced speakers almost collapse because they relied on a fistful of cards, which invariably get into the wrong order, or stick together, or descend from shaking hands like a small blizzard.

My technique is to type on a single page whatever statistical information I can't memorize, with maybe a few reminders to keep me on course. Then I use various colored felt marking pens, the ones that make a fat line but don't obscure the typing underneath, and put different ribbons of color through my cues. When I'm speaking and need to refer to the page, I have no difficulty picking out what comes next.

I also recommend delivering the speech beforehand,

even if your audience is only a three-year-old daughter. If you can tape it, and if you can bear to listen to it afterward (which I never can), you'll pick out speech faults you never realized you have. Even your own ear will inform you that you say "ahum" too frequently, or "you know." Newsman Edwin Newman and I once counted fourteen "you know's" during a ten-minute television speech given by a flabby-tongued politician.

Except when delivering something like a financial report, it's always more effective to leave the speech in your pocketbook. It's even true when you must introduce the guest speaker: memorize or jot down the highlights, boil it down to no more than a minute, and deliver it head-up.

It is wise to check the basic facts with the speaker himself before you start. You'll have obtained your biographical material from his lecture bureau, or from the local library or newspaper, but there could be an error. You don't want the situation where the speaker begins by correcting you, or sits behind you as you talk shaking his head negatively.

Remember it's an introduction that's required, not a testimonial fit for a memorial service. Academics in particular inflate their biographies with all of their appointments, degrees, and printed works; the audience is interested only in a rough idea of his qualifications.

Similarly, don't gush when thanking the speaker. Recently a woman thanking me after a lecture was so carried away that she cried, "All I can say is, *Thank God for Barbara Walters!*" I'm as fond of approval as anyone but it's unnerving to be deified. Keep the thanks simple and sincere, keying what you say to some part of the speech that especially caught your interest or something gracious about the speaker's style.

Above all, don't prepare the thank-you before you hear the speech. Nothing is more empty than a thank-you neatly typed the day before.

And don't rely, unless you're a consummate pro, on mechanical aids like tape recorded inserts or slides or musical effects. It's hilarious when a comedian does a skit about an imperturbable lecturer slowly dissolving as the slides appear upside down and in crazy order, but you won't find it funny at all if it happens to you.

I witnessed this kind of disaster not long ago when I appeared on a panel discussion with Gloria Steinem, one of the country's most sensitive writers and also, as I discovered, most nervous speakers. She had hoped to circumvent the problem of her panic by putting the speech on tape ahead of time. It was an ingenious idea, but the tape didn't work.

She devised an inventive solution: she gave the chairman some written questions and delivered her comments in the form of answers. It is much easier to be interviewed than to give a speech, or do the interviewing.

Remember that, if you're going to be interviewed on radio or television. Never script your answers in advance— all interviewers dislike that because it destroys the naturalness. Whenever it happens on *Today* that a guest brings scripted answers, we gently take his script away from him, sometimes right on the air. He's shocked at first but soon settles down to the spontaneous reactions that are much more effective.

Interviewers rarely go over their questions with guests in advance of the interview, for the same reasons. Without the element of the unexpected, interviews get a stale, stilted flavor. Most interviewers, however, do discuss with the guest the general areas that will be covered in the questions. I sometimes do this by telephone the day before the program, or else I take the guest aside for a few minutes just before we go on camera.

It is often a help if you write a short note to the researcher or writer preparing the questions and tell him what general areas you would most like to discuss and possibly a sample question or two. I welcome this kind of material because it makes my job easier.

Most interviewers will respect your request not to ask personal questions which may prove embarrassing. If you are concerned about something in particular, or perhaps prefer not to have a family reference, tell the interviewer frankly how you feel.

Keep your answers short: you can cover more territory that way. Hugh Downs and I often joke about Senator Mike Mansfield, who holds the world's title to taciturnity on television. You can ask Senator Mansfield the most complicated question such as, "Does the Democratic Party have as much future in the suburbs as in the city, in view of the inner-city unrest and the depersonalizing which comes with high density living?"

And he will answer, "No."

Ask the interviewer how much time has been allotted, and ask for some sort of time signal so you'll know when to wind up what you are saying. You don't want to be cut off while making your most important point. The system I use is to touch the guest out of camera range, with a hand on his knee or my foot against his, when we're running out of time. I warn him in advance about this, and instruct him not to be flustered when it happens—just finish his thought as succinctly as he can and let me end the interview by thanking him.

The trick has only failed me once. The *Today* program was in California and I was assigned to interview the veteran actor Leo G. Carroll, whose best-known role in recent years has been the cryptic boss in *The Man from U.N.C.L.E.* I explained my time signal device to him before the interview but Mr. Carroll isn't a young man and he promptly forgot. As I got my cue from the floor manager to wind up the interview, I reached over and touched Mr. Carroll lightly on the knee.

He drew himself up sharply. "Young woman!" he snapped. "What are you doing crawling up my thigh!" I explained weakly that it was my pre-arranged signal, and the interview mercifully ended, with the crew and cast of *Today* almost prostrate with laughter.

I have a final comment about public speaking—the obligatory opening joke too often seems contrived and phony to me. It is intended as a warm-up, to familiarize the audience with the speaker and arouse a certain affection. It has become a platform ritual but unless you really can tell a joke well, I distrust it.

Your opening remarks should be warm and friendly, just as you greet arriving guests. Mention that you're delighted to be there and, if there is a large turnout, how grateful you are that so many came. Really look at your audience and compliment them on how pretty they look or how fresh their spring dresses are.

I do, however, agree with the underlying principle of the opening joke, and I think it is a good idea to get even a serious speech off with a light touch. The humor, however, should be your own and not something out of a joke book. I'll illustrate by telling you what I sometimes say at the beginning of a speech, which is going to contain a number of references to my early-morning job on *Today* and its effect on my marriage. "If you can leave a man in bed at 5 A.M. and not hate him . . ." I say, and stop. "I mean, if you can leave your *husband* in bed at 5 A.M. and not hate him . . ."

Luckily, my husband doesn't attend my speeches.

Postscript
When All Else Fails

One of the pleasures of my life has been doing what are called "Prime Time Interview Specials." These are nice, fat, in-depth interviews with the superstars of the world, from presidents to athletes, but mostly with motion picture and television superstars. We've interviewed practically all of them—and we hope that when the viewer watches, he'll feel he really knows that person—moreover, that he can relate to that person. We want the viewer to feel as if he had a big, delicious meal—warm, satisfied, full, and cozy.

In order to do this, we sometimes ask over a hundred questions of our guest, not knowing exactly which one will turn him on or open the gates of intimacy. We try to stay away from very painful areas, but tears sometimes come as well as many laughs and some touching revelations. John Wayne telling us during his last interview that there was someone very close he wanted to pay tribute to, and then asking us to identify his secretary as his "dearest companion."

Bing Crosby admitting that if his daughter ever had an affair, he would not welcome her back in his home.

George Burns telling us of his conversations to this day with his late beloved wife, "Gracie."

Burt Reynolds saying that, more than anything else, he yearned to have a little boy look up and say, "Hello, Daddy."

Nancy Reagan, with tears in her eyes, discussing the assassination attempt on her husband.

Most of the time, the questions are tailored to the special individual I am talking to, but over the years my producer and I have found that certain questions can be used again and again to open a person up and have him think about himself and his life.

So here are some of those questions. Try them the next time you're stuck for conversation—or the next time you're trying for a closer relationship—or try them on yourself. Your answers may surprise you. But then, if you're really trying to talk with practically anybody about practically anything, you might want to start with the person you most want to know better—yourself.

What is the greatest misconception about you?
What was the toughest time in your life?
What was the best time in your life?
What is your biggest disappointment?
What do you like most about yourself? Least?
What are you most proud of?
Is there anything you want today that you do not have or cannot have?
If a fairy godmother offered you three wishes, what would you ask for?

If you had another chance, anything you'd do differently?
How would you like to be remembered?